2005

THE BEST 10-MINUTE PLAYS
FOR TWO ACTORS

Smith and Kraus'
Short Plays and 10-Minute Plays Collections

Christopher Durang Vol. I: 27 Short Plays

Frank D. Gilroy Vol. II: 15 One-Act Plays

Israel Horovitz Vol. I: 16 Short Plays

Romulus Linney 17 Short Plays

Terrence McNally Vol. I: 15 Short Plays

Lanford Wilson: 21 Short Plays

Act One Festival 1995: The Complete One-Act Plays

Act One Festival 1994: The Complete One-Act Plays

EST Marathon 1999: The Complete One-Act Plays

EST Marathon 1998: The Complete One-Act Plays

EST Marathon 1997: The Complete One-Act Plays

EST Marathon 1996: The Complete One-Act Plays

EST Marathon 1995: The Complete One-Act Plays

EST Marathon 1994: The Complete One-Act Plays

HB Playwrights Short Play Festival

    2003 The Subway Plays

    2002 The Beach Plays

    2001 The Hospital Plays

    2000 The Funeral Plays

    1999 The Airport Plays

    1998 The Museum Plays

    1997 The Motel Plays

Twenty One-Acts from 20 Years at the Humana Festival 1975–1995

The Women's Project and Productions Rowing to America and Sixteen Other Short Plays

8 TENS @ 8 Festival: 30 10-Minute Plays from the Santa Cruz Festivals I–VI

30 Ten-Minute Plays from the Actors Theatre of Louisville for 2 Actors

30 Ten-Minute Plays from the Actors Theatre of Louisville for 3 Actors

30 Ten-Minute Plays from the Actors Theatre of Louisville for 4, 5, and 6 Actors

2004: The Best 10-Minute Plays for Two Actors

2004: The Best 10-Minute Plays for Three or More Actors

2005
THE BEST 10-MINUTE PLAYS
FOR TWO ACTORS

Edited by D. L. Lepidus

CONTEMPORARY PLAYWRIGHT SERIES

A Smith and Kraus Book
Hanover, New Hampshire

Published by Smith and Kraus, Inc.
177 Lyme Road, Hanover, NH 03755
www.SmithandKraus.com / (888) 282-2881

First Edition: August 2007
10 9 8 7 6 5 4 3 2 1

Manufactured in the United States of America
Cover and Text Design by Julia Hill Gignoux, Freedom Hill Design
Cover photo by Amanda Embry: Brian Letscher and Danielle Quisenberry in *Cloudy* by Michael Griffo at Emerging Artists Theatre Fall EATfest of Short Plays 2005.

ISBN-10 1-57525-448-4
ISBN-13 978-1-57525-448-7
ISSN 1550-6754
Library of Congress Control Number: 2007930046

Contents

Introduction

The ten-minute play as an accepted dramatic form is a fairly recent development. Some would say that its popularity is a result of our diminished attention spans, which may be partially true. But here's how the genre came to be.

For several years, Actors Theatre of Louisville, under the leadership of Jon Jory, commissioned playwrights to write plays of short duration for performance by its apprentice company. This was a way for the theater to do something to help playwrights, but also it was a way to develop relationships with them, many of which bore fruit over the years as these writers went on to have full-length plays staged in Actors Theatre's famed Humana Festival.

Over the years, Actors Theatre built up quite a library of these short plays, all of them in manuscript. An editor at the play publisher Samuel French got the idea that maybe other theaters, actors, and students might be interested in these plays if they were made available to them. He managed to swing a deal for French to publish an anthology of Actors Theatre's best short plays, which they were now calling "ten-minute plays." This anthology was so successful that French has now published six such volumes, and most of the other publishers have followed suit, including Smith and Kraus, as its annual ten-minute plays anthologies will attest. Bills of ten-minute plays are now produced regularly, all over the world.

There are some who feel that the ten-minute play ought to be an opportunity for playwrights to experiment — with language, with form, with character, with subject matter. "The best" ten-minute plays are therefore the ones that depart the most from conventional drama. For the purposes of this series, here is how I define *best:* that which is most useful to people who will buy this book and produce these plays. Hard as it may be for dramaturges and suchlike, most people don't much care for plays that seek to reinvent the wheel. Well — once in a while they're OK, but most of the time audiences are shall we say unimpressed. Directors like the more experimental-type play, though, which gives them a better opportunity to call attention to their work than the more conventional, or realistic, play, which generally requires direction that is more or less invisible. I have therefore included several plays in a less conventional style that I hope will appeal to directors as well as to actors who like this kind of play.

Should you find a play (or plays) in this book that you want to produce, you will find information in the back on who to contact for performance rights.

D. L. Lepidus
Brooklyn, N.Y.

PLAYS FOR
ONE MAN
AND
ONE WOMAN

The First Time
Out of Bounds

P. SETH BAUER

CHARACTERS
    BOY
    GIRL

SETTING
    A field in New Hampshire

·   ·   ·

In the dark, two kids fumble around kissing each other. She speaks with a slight New Hampshire accent.

BOY: Umm . . .
GIRL: Uhh . . . Oh yeah.
BOY: Um.
GIRL: Oh yeah.
BOY: Ow.
GIRL: Huh?
BOY: Nothing, just — I can't get this —
GIRL: Hold on.
BOY: How does this thing work?
GIRL: Wait, just a minute, I'll do it.
    (She takes off her bra without removing her shirt. He sits there.)
    OK. It's off. What. Hello? Something wrong? Hello.
BOY: What no, everything's just . . .
GIRL: How ya doin'?
BOY: It's all good.
    (She kisses him some more and straddles him. He doesn't reciprocate.)
GIRL: Does my breath stink or something?
BOY: No. It's good. It smells good — like camel lights and spearmint.
GIRL: That's the binaca. Want some.
BOY: No I'm —
GIRL: Sure?
BOY: I'm good.
    (Short pause.)
    You like this place?
GIRL: Yeah.
    (Short pause.)
    You want me to suck your cock.
BOY: What?

GIRL: I'm wicked good at it.

BOY: No I'm fine, it's all, you know later — whatever — let's just sit here, look at the sky.

GIRL: 'Kay.

BOY: Isn't that amazing?

GIRL: Yep.

BOY: So many suns. I heard the other day that we can see galaxies that have gone a million years only cuz of the speed of light, we're only now seeing them.

GIRL: How old are you?

BOY: Why? Seventeen.

GIRL: Seventeen years old and you say no to a blow job.

BOY: No I'm not saying no, it's just — my mind is . . .

GIRL: Am I not cute?

BOY: You're totally cute.

GIRL: I'm not a slut alright. I don't go down on every boy I see.

BOY: Sure I know.

GIRL: You know?

BOY: No I don't mean I "know" know like I know something or other — I just meant . . . I know what you mean.

GIRL: Oh.

BOY: And you are "wicked cute."

GIRL: I am.

BOY: I know. Totally.

GIRL: You like these?

(She exposes her garter straps.)

BOY: Oh yeah. Yes, I — yes.

GIRL: Got 'em special at a vintage clothing store down Nashua. My sister took me. I had no idea ladies wore these things back then but there was like a ton of them. Totally old and lacy.

BOY: Well they all did actually. I mean it was pretty common for stockings to come up just above the knee like this.

GIRL: For real?

BOY: Yeah. That way they had a long sexy garter that went all the way to here.

(He traces her leg up her skirt. They start to fool around some more. He stops.)

BOY: Sorry.

GIRL: Jesum Crow. The fuck's wrong with you?

BOY: I just don't know you that well —

GIRL: What's to know?

BOY: I mean I don't even know your birthday.

GIRL: You wanna know my birthday 'fore you fuck me.
> *(She laughs at him.)*

BOY: It's getting late. I better get you home.

GIRL: June the 4th.

BOY: The 4th of June.

GIRL: Think I'm making it up.

BOY: But what's today?

GIRL: The fifth.

BOY: Today's the fifth? So like yesterday was your birthday.

GIRL: You are some kinda math genius.

BOY: Well happy birthday.

GIRL: Right.

BOY: And many happy returns.

GIRL: What is that?

BOY: Something my grandpa used to say.

GIRL: Oh. Yeah.

BOY: He used to say always wish a lady many happy returns and never ask their age.

GIRL: I'm fifteen.

BOY: You're fifteen?

GIRL: And not shy about my age.

BOY: You just turned fifteen.

GIRL: What'd you think I was?

BOY: I don't know — I just didn't think you were that age — I mean um, aren't you a junior?

GIRL: I skipped kindergarten.

BOY: Well that's great. Kindergarten's such a waste of time anyway, you didn't miss much. So how long have you been doing this?

GIRL: Doing what?

BOY: I don't know, I mean you know . . . dating and . . .

GIRL: Not getting laid?

BOY: Yeah, I mean . . . I guess I'm wondering how many years since you lost your . . .

GIRL: Cherry?

BOY: It's none of my . . .

GIRL: Well how would your grandpa ask me?

BOY: It would never come up.

GIRL: You think I'm too young for you.

BOY: I'm not judging you.

GIRL: Right.

(She starts getting dressed.)

BOY: What are you doing?

GIRL: What's it look like?

BOY: You don't have to go.

GIRL: Fuck you.

BOY: What? Let's just —

GIRL: What did you expect?! You know, you take me out to dinner, a dinner like that. Somehow you get us wine in a little pitcher and everything. There's even a fire in the friggin' fireplace! Violins are playing, the whole bit. Then you take me to see a play, not a movie, not bowling, a play. I never seen a play before 'cept when I was a kid and they took our class down to the Palace Theater to see Rumplestiltskin and what-not. We walk by the lake. You hold my hand. We look at the Goddamn stars for hours. Then you take me to a friggin' ditch by the side of the road and not fuck me. I don't know what this is and I don't know if you're some kinda funny or what not —

BOY: Wait what?

GIRL: Just nothing —

BOY: What made you say that?

GIRL: I gotta go.

BOY: Hold on.

GIRL: See you in study hall.

BOY: I'm not a faggot.

GIRL: Yeah well . . . Good for you.

BOY: I know what people say but it's all bullshit.

GIRL: Merry Christmas.

BOY: Where are you going?

GIRL: The fuck do you care.

(He shrugs. Pause.)

BOY: You are totally cute, you are. When I asked you out I didn't think you'd say yes. A long time, I wanted to take you out. I just didn't want to go to the mall or movies and what not. I wanted to do something different. I just didn't have enough money to . . . it just took me a little while to save is all. And I'm wicked sorry about the ditch. My mom's home and I didn't have enough money for whatever and I know nobody comes here is all so I thought we could have you know — privacy. See I been think-ing about this night a lot, for a while. Wondering, you know . . . what it'd be like to get with you. And now you're here with me and I'm fuck-ing it all up I know. Believe me it's not intentional.

GIRL: Is this your first time?

BOY: No. Not really. I've had sex a few times. Nothing major. I just — it all sort of —

GIRL: Sucked.

BOY: It was just no big deal.

GIRL: Good sex is hard to do right.

BOY: Plus you throw in pregnancy and AIDS and what not.

GIRL: Pre-ejaculation.

BOY: Right. And I don't know . . . My grandpa says I should wait til I'm married and then it'll all be fine, no worries and anything else is like out-of-bounds or whatever.

GIRL: I'm not a slut.

BOY: I know you're not.

GIRL: I just like you.

BOY: For real?

GIRL: No I'm faking it.

BOY: So you wanna sit here and look at the sky a little more.

GIRL: Any more beers.

BOY: Probably warm though.

GIRL: No big whoop. Where'd you get these?

BOY: Off a guy I know, works down the Extra Mart.

GIRL: Cool.

BOY: Yeah. He'll Probably get fired though you know.

GIRL: Big time.

BOY: Yeah.

GIRL: Can you get some more of these 'fore he gets fired?

BOY: Probably.

GIRL: Cuz maybe we can party at my house when my parents go the Cape.

BOY: Oh.

GIRL: We got a pool.

BOY: Nice.

GIRL: No biggy.

BOY: When they go to the Cape?

GIRL: Usually August.

BOY: Cool. *(Slight pause.)* It's June now though right?

GIRL: Yep.

BOY: So . . . August.

GIRL: Yeah.

BOY: Cool.

> *(They drink beer. Lights.)*

 END OF PLAY

Bethlehem, PA

Suzanne Bradbeer

For Chris Campbell

Bethlehem, PA was first presented by Vital Theatre Company, Stephen Sunderlin, Artistic Director, Sharon Fallon, Managing Director. Directed by Linda Ames Key, with Chris Campbell and Chance Muehleck. Subsequently produced by City Theatre's Summer Shorts Festival, 2004. Directed by Barbara Lowery, with Camille Carida and Gregg Weiner.

CHARACTERS
    BUNNY: thirties
    JOE: thirties

SETTING
    A backyard in Bethlehem, PA. After midnight.

• • •

Lights up on a man squatting by a freshly covered grave, shovel at his side. It is a very bright moon. He picks up a bottle at his side, opens it. Behind his back a figure flits past in the darkness, scarf and dress flowing Isadora-like behind her. He looks up and then behind, sensing something, but she's already out of sight. Must have been nothing, his imagination. He takes a swig from the bottle. The figure flits by again coming from the opposite direction, and this time he catches a glance of her flowing garments as she disappears stage left.

JOE: What the hell was that?
    (The figure starts to flit past again, oblivious. She has almost passed offstage when the man grabs his shovel, and stands.)
JOE: *(Continued.) (As he stands.)* What the hell is going on?
    (The figure stops suddenly, still as a statue. She screams.)
JOE: *(Continued. Startled.)* Jesus.
    (She screams again.)
JOE: *(Continued.)* Sorry!
    (She screams again.)
JOE: *(Continued.)* Whoa.
BUNNY: You gave me the fright of me life, Oh My God! Rising out of the ground like that, like the King himself! That's one for the books, wheeee the adrenaline rush, I feel a little flushed —
JOE: Yeah well. Party's over.
BUNNY: Now this is pretty funny, isn't it? Because Harvey was *just* saying — that's my landlord — you know him, right, the guy with the eye? Anyway, he was talking about my next-door neighbor and how he was quiet, keeps to himself — and that has to be you, right, so nice to meet you, although they do say, and I hope you won't take this the wrong way, but they do say that it's often the *quiet* ones, the nice quiet loners who are exactly the people with a backyard full of bodies, you ever noticed that? I took a sociology class at PCC — Piedmont Community College, that's back where I'm from, and although we didn't talk about mass murderers

per se — Wow. You sure are handsome — hi. *(Beat.)* Pardon moi, Monsieur, you can return the compliment if you want.

JOE: What.

BUNNY: Say I'm pretty or whatever.

JOE: Are you?

BUNNY: What are you blind, you can't see me? I'm gorgeous! Right?! I'm just teasing you, it's a little game I used to play with my husband: "You're handsome," "No, *you're* gorgeous." It was a lot of laughs. Back in the day . . . *(Beat. In her distraction she has dropped one of her prettiest scarves, maybe one that has tiny little bells and sequins. However she doesn't notice this.)* So Harvey also said you used to be in steel, and now you work for the Parks Department, right? He didn't say anything about handsome — or blind for that matter — oh God you *can* see me can't you? Because that would be exactly my luck, I make a little joke or I stick up for myself for once and somehow I end up dropping that poor baby on it's head or asking someone who can't see "Are you blind" and they *are*. I'm sorry, I'm babbling. You're standing there all, Big, and, with that sort of Me Tarzan thing going on —

JOE: *(Mumbling.)* I'm not blind, you nutty, nut.

BUNNY: What?

JOE: I'M NOT BLIND!

BUNNY: What a relief — hey — since we're both already out here and you *can* see and everything, would you mind taking a little look at this dance piece I've been working on? I've been dying for an audience.

JOE: Who are you?

BUNNY: Oh wow, thanks for asking, you're the first person to ask me that since I moved here. I'm fine pretty much, it's been a very tough year, but I've really turned things around for myself lately, and I'm feeling much better about everything —

JOE: I said, *who* are you?

BUNNY: OH. I'm your next-door neighbor, I just moved in next door. *(Under her breath.)* And also I'm *fine*, thanks so much for asking.

JOE: Look, you're in my yard. This is my private yard. Would you mind just, taking it back to wherever it is you came from, and leaving me alone?

BUNNY: I came from next door, but — OK, OK — you don't have to watch me, but do you mind if I just rehearse a little, back here, I won't bother you, I promise, it's just that my yard is kind of spooky and cramped —

JOE: All these yards are the same size.

BUNNY: Plus I've been out here for the past three nights and I've gotten used to the terrain. I didn't think it would bother anyone —

JOE: Oh but it does. It really does.

(The moon has come from behind a cloud, bright. Perhaps an owl hoots, or some other nighttime sound, and is it her imagination or did he suddenly get a lot bigger, looming over her? She seems to notice the grave for the first time.)

BUNNY: What, what's that.

JOE: . . . Nothing.

BUNNY: That's a grave.

JOE: Huh.

BUNNY: That's a fresh grave.

JOE: Huh.

BUNNY: Oh my God.

JOE: It's nothing for you to worry about.

BUNNY: Of course it isn't. I'm not worried. *(She raises her fist in a black power salute.)* Rock on! *(She starts to walk away backwards, still facing him, then turns forward, takes a few steps, and then turns back again suddenly, as if to catch him stalking her. He isn't.)* I can barely even see you. I'd never be able to point you out in a lineup. Even if I wanted to, which I don't. I'm a little blind myself if you want to know the truth.

JOE: Really.

(As she continues to back away she trips on her scarves or dress or something, falls.)

BUNNY: Oomfh.

(He stares at her, shovel still at his side. Maybe he raises it, just a little. She scrambles to her feet and hurries off. He watches her go. Turning back to the grave, he stands looking at it, considering. He picks a stick or stone from the freshly turned earth and tosses it to the side. He takes a swig from the bottle. He sees her fallen scarf, picks it up. Meanwhile she is hovering at the edge of the yard, looking for the missing scarf. He is soon aware of her presence, and she is aware that he is aware. He holds out the missing scarf at arm's length, like it's a dirty sock.)

JOE: You might as well come get it.

BUNNY: *(She approaches, taking the scarf gingerly. She considers the grave.)* It's kind of a small grave.

JOE: You don't need much space when some of the key body parts are missing.

BUNNY: Oh no you don't, I've got your number now.

JOE: *(Beat.)* Good night.

BUNNY: *(She looks at him a moment, then says gently.)* Was it, did you lose a pet?

JOE: That's none of your business.

BUNNY: *(This is the last straw.)* WHAT A FUCKING CRANK!!!

JOE: *Whoa.*

BUNNY: What are you, some kind of, of, of, you know, automated, auto . . . person? I'm sorry, I must seem really selfish to want a little company — I've just been so crazed for some human contact — I mean I chose this city because it sounded friendly and I'd never been here and more importantly, I'd never danced here — and I've danced almost everywhere, Buster. Featured performer, had my own act, on the road all over the country — yeah, that's right, I was a *stripper.* Oh fuck me. I said it. I told myself I wouldn't tell anyone, at least not right away — people get the wrong idea — but noooo, it always just wants to jump out of me. I've already told the landlord, the lady at the Stop and Shop, the gas-station attendant, and now you. *(Beat.)* OK, well, thanks for the scarf back. *(She stands above the grave, waves her scarf in adieu.)* Good-bye, whoever, whatever you are.

JOE: *(Reluctantly.)* . . . It's my bunny.

BUNNY: —— ——

JOE: She died.

BUNNY: —— ——

JOE: She was old.

BUNNY: —— ——

JOE: Her name was Bunny.

BUNNY: Bunny?

JOE: What. It's a good name.

BUNNY: No, no, I know —

JOE: She'd been ill and old and then she died tonight, and I have to work early tomorrow, so I figured I'd better go ahead and get her in the ground. You have all the facts now, you happy?

BUNNY: I bet she was a nice bunny.

JOE: She was. She was a very good bunny.

BUNNY: What was she like?

JOE: She was brown and gray and had a highly developed sense of irony.

BUNNY: You know what? You hold on Buster, I just want to get something from my yard real quick. I'll be right back.

JOE: What?! No — not right back. No, good night, good night already! *(Calling out.)* No̱t right back!!

(But she has run off and he is alone. Perhaps a neighborhood-y sound here, a dog barking, someone calling . . . she runs back on, carrying two votive candles in holders.)

BUNNY: I'm not staying, I just wanted to leave these candles with you.

JOE: OK, yeah — see — that's very nice, but I don't really go for that hippy-incense-vibrators kind of scenario.

BUNNY: They're just *candles*. They're for Bunny. To light her through the night.

JOE: *(Embarrassed.)* Oh. Thanks, yeah, thanks a lot.

BUNNY: Here, let me light them for you.

JOE: No, that's all right, really, I appreciate it . . . I just prefer to be . . . *(She has lit the candles.)*

JOE: *(Continued.)* . . . alone . . .
(She puts them by the grave; perhaps there's a friendly night sound.)

JOE: *(Continued.) (Moved, in spite of himself.)* Thanks. That's nice, it is. I appreciate it, real nice. *(Feeling awkward.)* Aren't they pretty.

BUNNY: They are, aren't they? Bunny was a good and lovely bunny. A truly lovely bunny was Bunny.
(They stand reverently for a beat. He wipes his nose.)

JOE: Actually Bunny was kind of a funny-looking bunny. What with her hunchback and just the one ear. Not to mention that recurring case of mange, whoa. But you're right, she was lovely, in her way. And she had a fighting spirit. The guys at work thought I should just leave her where I found her all those years ago, a ragamuffin beat-up little thing. But I couldn't do that. She was just a baby; lost, bleeding, alone in the world, making that little bunny whimper . . . *(Perhaps he makes the sound of a little bunny whimper.)* I took her home, nursed her back to health. And she saw *me* through the two worst events of my adult life: my divorce, and when the Pirates played their final game at Three River Stadium and *lost* to the Cubs, 10-9.

BUNNY: That's so beautiful. *(A little emotional.)* I hate funerals. *(Referring to his bottle.)* What is that? Jack?

JOE: Yeah . . .

BUNNY: Yummy.

JOE: *(Oh what the hell . . .)* You want some? *(Offers the Jack Daniels.)*

BUNNY: Thank you. *(She takes a big swig, passes it back.)* It's just all so sad isn't it? All of it.

JOE: It is. I personally don't like good-byes of any kind. So I usually don't even say hello. *(He takes a swig.)*

BUNNY: Oh . . . yeah. I didn't even like saying good-bye to stripping, but I'd been doing it for a very long time and I was worn out. I'm not old really, I mean Julia Roberts is older than me by a good year, but the business is getting younger and meaner, and I was getting older and . . . meaner . . . I love dancing, that's the crazy thing. I always created stories with my dancing, I mean the guys, the *guys* . . . well, the guys didn't know that I'm sure, but each song had a story for me. Anyway, I've been trying to think of ways to continue dancing, not like before, but, in other ways. *(Beat.)*

Who am I kidding? You know? Who cares. I'm such a dope: I wanted to start over where I didn't know anyone, and here I am and, *(A little teary.)* I don't know anyone . . .

JOE: *(Long beat. He takes a swig.)* Why don't you show me your, whatever it is.

BUNNY: *(Wiping her eyes.)* Oh-No-No-No, I've bothered you enough — well OK! *(Suddenly hopeful.)* You know, maybe it's just the thing. I think, I hope it's kind of inspiring.

JOE: Are you going to take your clothes off?

BUNNY: Oh no, it's not *that* kind of thing.

JOE: Because that would be kind of inspiring.

BUNNY: *(As she's getting ready, loosening up, arranging her scarves, whatever.)* I'll just show you a taste, the most polished section so far. My idea is to present this to the powers that be, as soon as I figure out who they are. OK, so they call this the "Christmas City" right, and this is — ta da! — a Christmas Pageant Dance for the Birth of Jesus. Can I have another swig of that? Thanks. Except, OK, it's kind of radical: It's a sort of fantasia ode-to-*Joseph* 'cause I for one, always thought Joseph gets kind of short shrift with all that Babe-in-a-Manger Broohaha, you know? I mean Joseph, *Joseph*, look at him. Here he is, he's a plain guy, right? I mean, I know he's descended from kings and everything, but aren't we all when you get right down to it? So he's a plain guy, no philosopher or deep thinker or whatever, and here *she* comes — and this is back in the day remember — here she comes saying she's pregnant *by-the-hand-of-God*, and I mean, what would *you* say to that? What would anybody, angel or no angel? But he stood by her. And I just find that so, beautiful. Don't you?

JOE: —— ——

BUNNY: Everyone else, it's all Jesus this and Mary that, and I appreciate them, I do, but Joseph, he's the one that really speaks to me in all this. So I'm hoping they will use my tribute to him in part of the festival this year. Tradition or no tradition, there must be room in the Christmas City for a little Joseph — I mean, shake it up people!!

JOE: Huh. *(She waits, seems to be expecting something.)* Go ahead.

BUNNY: *(Suddenly nervous.)* OK, I have one question before I show you.

JOE: What?

BUNNY: How do you feel about Barry White?

JOE: I feel good about him.

BUNNY: I thought so! I just wanted to, if you didn't like Barry, I, and I hate to sound harsh, but I just wouldn't think you'd have anything to say to me. Not that my piece is in any way Barry-y, but, he's kind of my barometer for cultural criticism. (*A deep breath.*) OK, here we go. (*She dances a kind of loopy, sexy, charming dance. Obviously full of meaning, but God knows what. After however long seems right, she's done, and flushed from having exposed herself so deeply. And he "got it," somehow, on some level. Speechless for a moment, he just nods his head emphatically. She looks at him expectantly, nervously.*)

JOE: (*Beat.*) It was *very* inspiring.

BUNNY: Really? Thank you. Thank you. It's about love, in the end. I mean, of course it is, that's what it's *all* about, don't you think?

JOE: —— ——

BUNNY: Did you, but what did you think of the Three Wise Men, did that part work for you?

JOE: (*Having no idea what's she's talking about.*) Yeah.

BUNNY: I bet you didn't notice that one of them was a woman, did you? 'Fess up.

JOE: No.

BUNNY: In my piece, one of the Wise Men is a Wise *Woman*. It's my little "statement." But that's not clear yet is it? It's very hard to get that across, if people aren't expecting it. I'll have to do some more work on that part.

(*Beat, as they're taking each other in.*)

So . . . thanks . . . I'll, I should leave you alone now. Right? *Finally?*

JOE: (*Suddenly, with passion.*) You should keep up with that dancing. I mean, in whatever new directions you want to take it: Christmas Pageants, Easter Parades, Bar Mitzvahs, or what have you. You're very talented.

BUNNY: (*Touched.*) Thank you. (*Beat.*) So, good night. (*She hesitates, turns to go back to her own yard.*)

JOE: Hey, I don't even know your name. I'm Joe.

BUNNY: Allison. But everyone calls me Bunny. (*She shrugs.*)

JOE: (*Beat.*) Hello Bunny.

BUNNY: . . . Hello.

(*They look at each other, and at the lights flickering. Curtain.*)

END OF PLAY

The Ghost of Red Roses

DAVID CIRONE

CHARACTERS
   HAL: late forties
   SANDY: early forties

SETTING
   A bar in southwest Georgia. Near two o'clock in the morning.

. . .

Sandy and Hal sit at a bar. The jukebox plays lively country/western songs.
It's nearly closing time. Hal is still in his factory uniform, fresh from work-
ing the night shift. Sandy is dressed for a night out — she has big hair and
big earrings and a brightly colored blouse. There's a single red rose in a small
vase in front of Hal. They've been talking and drinking for a while.

SANDY: You know, I've been meaning to tell you — that's a really pretty rose
   you got there.
HAL: Thank you.
SANDY: I mean, I sorta had my eye on it since I sat down here . . .
HAL: Yeah?
SANDY: . . . and I've been sitting here *a while now.*
HAL: Uh-huh.
SANDY: And?
HAL: . . . And?
SANDY: Well, I'm wondering if you're gonna give it to me.
   (He smiles, laughs to himself.)
SANDY: Why not?
HAL: We just met.
SANDY: It's Valentine's Day. Ain't you supposed to give flowers?
HAL: I suppose.
SANDY: So . . . Hal . . . what are you waiting for?
   (She gives him her cutest smile.)
HAL: You are too much!
SANDY: No? Aw, you're gonna break my heart!
HAL: I don't know about that!
SANDY: *(Pouting.)* It's true!
HAL: Well, true or not . . .
   (He trails off.)
SANDY: Yeah . . . ? It ain't doing nobody no good sitting there by itself.
HAL: It ain't by itself. It's with me.

SANDY: Hal, I didn't get any flowers today, not one.

HAL: I don't believe that for a minute.

SANDY: It's true! Cryin' shame, right?

HAL: Well, this here flower's promised to somebody special.

SANDY: Can't be that special. She ain't here with you, I am!

HAL: Yeah, that's true — but it's somebody I love, with all my heart.

SANDY: *(Loud.) With all your . . . ?* Oh, now wait a minute! Come on!

HAL: *(Grinning at her excitement.)* I mean it. Absolutely, I mean that.

SANDY: With all your heart?

HAL: *(Drinking.)* Yeah!

SANDY: *(Sarcastic.)* Well prove it!

HAL: What . . . ?

> *(His mood changes.)*
>
> Sorry, what did you say?

SANDY: I said prove it. Show me!

HAL: "Prove it?"

SANDY: Yes! I — speaking on behalf of my gloriously superior gender — I would like to know what "all my heart" looks like. That's what you said, right?

> *(He looks at her with real amazement.)*

HAL: I'm sorry, what was your name again?

SANDY: Sandy.

HAL: Sandy.

> *(Pause.)*
>
> Wow . . . I just can't believe you said that. Man — man, that is, that is really strange.

SANDY: Well, no offense, but that seems to me like an impossibly big thing. "All your heart?" Please! I've heard that from men so many times in my life, I can't even count!

HAL: So . . . ?

SANDY: *So . . .* it can't be true!

HAL: It is. I did.

SANDY: Wait a minute — did? Like done?

HAL: Yeah. Yeah, she left me.

SANDY: Oh, now this is too much! She left you and you're still keeping this for her? Hal!

> *(Drinks.)*
>
> "Let me tell you, I'm over it honey!" I don't believe it! Any man says that to me, I know he's lost in some poetry book he read back in the ninth grade, he ain't in the real world no more!

(Beat.)

SANDY: I hurt your feelings?

HAL: No, it's OK.

(Beat.)

SANDY: What you thinking?

HAL: My wife and I used to come here. That same spot where you're sitting, that's where she used to sit. We'd drink all night. She drank me under the table so many times . . . ! Made me feel like a little kid, sometimes.
(Rolls up sleeve.)
Look here, look right here — I got this tattoo on my arm with her name on it. Right here. And that's permanent, ain't one of them rub-on ones like my brother's kids are wearing. No, that's *real ink*, right there in my own skin — took a long time and it *hurt*. Only tattoo I ever got. So that's *her* arm, forever.

SANDY: Looks to me like it's yours. You're the one using it, you're the one carrying it around with you, here and there and everywhere . . .

HAL: But yeah, that's what I'm saying! You're saying you don't believe it and I'm saying it's true. I *gave* this arm to her. Everywhere I go, people are gonna see her name on it. Ain't that what love is? Love . . . love is . . .
(Searching for the words.)
. . . you know, love is giving something of yours to somebody else. *That's* love — and that's what I've been doing, ever since I met her. I been giving, giving *everything*, and if I had more, I'd give her more. If I had something I could give, anything she could want or if I could dream of something more . . . I would give it. I know I would give it. And that's what I mean. That's all my heart.
(Pause.)
And, well, if you can come up with something better than that . . .
(Pause.)
Like what you just said, saying "prove it." Well, she used to tell me, "Hal, you say that to me every morning and every night — 'I love you with all my heart.'" And then I'd say, "But I do, sugar — I love you as much as I can. I feel like my heart's gonna swell up and burst every time I look at you." And she'd say, "OK. Prove it."
(Laughs.)
I mean, I'm *dying* here trying to prove it to that woman! Got her that color TV for the living room, got her them surprise flowers for her birthday . . . You know, I once went up and down this town and bought *every red rose* I could find for her birthday — laid them out all around the house, on the porch, in the bedroom . . . she loved them roses so much. I looked

at her that day, looked her right in the eye and said, "Did I prove it yet, honey?" And she smiled . . . said "You're getting there, Hal." *(Grins.)* She had the sweetest smile.

SANDY: Must have been a great woman.

HAL: She was. She was.

SANDY: So why'd she leave you?

(Beat.)

HAL: Hey, you want another drink?

SANDY: Nah, I'm good. I think I'm gonna sip on this one 'til they throw us out.

HAL: Is it that late?

SANDY: Yep.

HAL: Is it two o'clock already?

SANDY: Yep. You know, I had a man like you once, nearly made me believe the sun rose and set over me. He was a sweet one, but sort of . . . I don't know, sort of "off," if you know what I mean.

(Looks over at him.)

Hey, you OK?

HAL: Yeah, I'm fine.

SANDY: You're looking a little teary-eyed all of a sudden. You want a tissue or something?

HAL: No, no, I'm fine. I'm OK.

SANDY: Don't go all mushy on me, now. I'm having a good time tonight.

HAL: Yeah. *(Looking to change the subject.)* So — what's new with you? *(A little laugh.)* Sorry, just trying to lighten it up. Don't wanna be a downer.

SANDY: No, you're doing just fine.

(Pause.)

Listen, can I ask you . . . ? I don't wanna bring it up again if you don't want, but . . . well, I know I'm a lost cause, I'm sort of spoiled on the whole thing, but . . .

(Gently.) Well, for *her* — for your wife — did you ever . . . ? Did you ever prove it to her?

(A pause. He looks at her for a long time.)

HAL: *(Keeping his smile.)* My wife, um . . . She had cancer, and well, when she died, I was there with her. I made sure I was with her all the time, and well, I'm holding her hand, and she's looking at me. She didn't talk much, 'cuz of the morphine, but — you know, I know this is sad, but I can't help smiling when I think about her — she wasn't talking much, but she looked at me, and said — in the *clearest voice*, she said — "You keep trying, Hal. You keep trying, and when you get it right, I'll come back. I'll come back to you." I ain't never forgot that. And if you think I don't believe her, you're wrong, 'cuz I do. I'm still trying, Sandy. I don't know how much good I'm doing right here, tonight, sitting here in this bar, but . . .

(Pause.) I am trying.

(A long pause.)

SANDY: That was some story.

HAL: Yeah, yeah, I'm sorry I didn't mean to . . .

SANDY: No, I mean it was a good story.

HAL: Thank you.

SANDY: You believe in angels, Hal?

HAL: Yeah, I believe in angels.

SANDY: You know them stories they tell you in Sunday School, about how you better be nice to everybody 'cuz you never know who's an angel and who's not?

HAL: Yeah, I remember all that.

SANDY: Something tells me that your wife . . . Something tells me that you've got an angel looking out for you, Hal. You've got a good heart. I can tell that about you. I could tell that the moment I sat down and we started talking.

HAL: You think so? I don't know . . . maybe. I don't know.

SANDY: Yeah, I think so.

(The jukebox comes on again, playing a country/western love song. She finishes her drink, and pulls out her purse. She leaves a few bills on the bar.

SANDY: This last one's on me.

HAL: Awful kind of you. Thank you.

(A pause.)

SANDY: *(Deep breath — looks him square in the eye.)* So.

(There was a lot of meaning in that "So." It gets his attention.)

HAL: Hm? Beg your pardon?

SANDY: *(Another deep breath — still looking dead on.)* So . . . ?

(She's really giving him the look now, grinning like the Cheshire Cat.)

HAL: Are you . . . ? Are you trying to . . . ?

(Blushing like a little boy — she doesn't blink.)

Aw . . . Sandy, come on . . . !

SANDY: *(Toying shamelessly.)* "Come on," what?

(The same attitude.) Soooo . . . ?

HAL: Aww . . .

SANDY: "Aww . . . " Come on, maybe I can be a gift for you. Give you something happy today.

HAL: That would be nice. I mean, you are . . . you are *something* . . .

SANDY: Yes, I am.

HAL: . . . but . . .

SANDY: What? You got something better to do tonight?

HAL: You mean, like right now . . .

SANDY: Right now.

HAL: *(Grinning, embarrassed.)* Sandy . . .

SANDY: *(Grinning back.)* Hal . . .

HAL: You're a good-looking woman — I mean, you're a very — *very* — good-looking woman, and you're very nice, very sweet . . .

SANDY: . . . *and* it's Valentine's Day!

HAL: *(Nods.)* And it's Valentine's Day, but . . .
(She touches his hand softly. He stares down at it.)

HAL: You're very pretty.

SANDY: Thank you. You're very sweet.

HAL: I guess . . . I mean, I *could* . . .

SANDY: Yes, you could.
(Beat.)

HAL: I can't. Really — thank you, but I can't.

SANDY: You sure? Been sitting here, listening to that jukebox play Elvis and Merle Haggard all night, talking you up, hoping you'd come home with me . . .
(Pause.) I mean, you're passing up something special here!
(She's still holding his hand.)

SANDY: *(One last try.)* Hal . . .
(Softer.) Hal, come on . . .

HAL: *(Laughs.)* Really, it's sweet of you to offer, but . . . God, you are a fine-looking woman.

SANDY: So what's holding you up? Don't tell me lil' Cupid don't got no arrows left . . . ?

HAL: OK, right . . . right. Heh, that's funny.
(Pause.) Look . . . she's still got me, you know? I'm still . . .
(Finding the words.) She's still my girl. That's all I can say. She's still my girl. *(Taps chest.)* Everything I got in here is tied up with her. And you're too nice to just . . . I just couldn't. I'm sorry.

SANDY: *(Playfully.)* Last chance . . .

HAL: You don't give up, do you?

SANDY: *(Poorly pretending.)* OK! Fine! Fine! Send a lonely, nearly middle-aged woman home all by her lonesome! I tell you, there's no justice in this world . . . !

(Winks at him.) . . . know what I mean?

HAL: *(Smiling.)* Thanks again, Sandy. For that last drink.

SANDY: You got it, Sugar.

(She gets up, fumbling with her purse.)

SANDY: Good night. Happy Valentine's Day, Hal.

HAL: Happy Valentine's Day, Sandy.

(She kisses him lightly on the forehead, then exits. Hal stares after her, then down at his drink.)

HAL: Hmm . . . *(Shakes his head.)* "Prove it . . . "

(He takes the rose out of the vase, twirling it around in his fingers. A pause. He stares at that rose for a long time.)

HAL: Goddamn.

(The jukebox keeps playing as the lights fade.)

END OF PLAY

Strange Attractions

DAVID EPSTEIN

The full-length family drama *Strange Attractions* opened to New York audiences in 2004 and was produced by Invisible City Theater Company. The author directed the original production. The following excerpt has appeared in a number of one-act festivals — most notably, the ICTC annual short play festival; as well as at the Artist's at Work short play series.

CHARACTERS
    LINA HILFORD: twenty
    DARREN JACOBS: Lina's tutor

SETTING
    Surburbia

• • •

Suburbia. It is a hot summer night. A dumpy living room looks into an exposed kitchen. Lina Hilford, twenty, enters from the foyer. Her clothes reek of "antiestablishment": spiked dog collar, anarchy T-shirt, dyed black hair. Darren Jacobs follows her in wearing a plaid shirt and blue jeans. With his congenial face, Darren may one day be the leader of the Free World. But for now, he is a tutor.

DARREN: Where do you want to work?

LINA: If I wanted to work I wouldn't need a tutor, would I?

(He sets his backpack on the kitchen table. Lina plops on the couch and doodles in a sketchpad.)

DARREN: Do you have your book?

LINA: Oh, there's a book? No wonder I'm so far behind.

DARREN: I have an extra.

(He grabs the text from his stack then stares at her.)

LINA: What?!

DARREN: We should get started. Why don't you come over here and you can tell me where you're up to.

LINA: I'm fine where I am.

DARREN: Can I say something?

LINA: I'm all ears, Professor.

DARREN: Darren is fine.

LINA: Well, actually, I'd be more comfortable if I could call you Professor Darren, if that would be all right?

DARREN: Mathematics can be a lot of fun, Lina. Did you know that? There's nothing to be afraid of.

LINA: Does this look like the face of fear?

DARREN: I don't mean afraid on a visceral level. I'm trying to explain that people don't usually like math because the laws seem so rigid. But once you learn the formula, it can be very exciting.

LINA: Darren?

DARREN: That's right.

LINA: I'm going to be honest with you before I fall asleep from boredom.

DARREN: OK.

LINA: You are my third tutor this semester and they've all tried what you are trying.

DARREN: What am I trying?

LINA: To get me riled up about things that have no bearing on my life. Trust me. You'll be saving yourself the trouble if you packed up your magic rocks and went back to whatever library it is that spawned you.

DARREN: Who pays for your classes?

LINA: That's none of your business.

DARREN: Come on. Who pays? Parents? You're obviously not on scholarship.

LINA: Fuck you.

DARREN: *(Zero hesitation.)* Fuck you. I'm just wondering whose money you're wasting.

LINA: Who pays for your classes you nosy prick?

DARREN: As a matter of fact I do.

LINA: Oh, of course. I should have known. Hit me with a car and call me Steven Eagle.

DARREN: Steven — I'm sorry . . . Who?

LINA: Steven Eagle.

DARREN: Who is Steven Eagle?

LINA: The math guy.

DARREN: Which math guy?

LINA: The one in the wheelchair.

DARREN: You mean Stephen Hawking?

LINA: No. I mean Steven Eagle.

DARREN: No. You mean Stephen Hawking. You're mixing your birds.

LINA: Well who-ever-the-fuck. He is in a wheelchair.

DARREN: Yes, he is, and it's not because he got hit by a car.

(Darren opens his book and begins to read. Lina can hardly bear the silence.)

LINA: Hello?!

DARREN: What?

LINA: What are you doing?

DARREN: My homework.

LINA: Uh, no one is keeping you. You can leave any time.

DARREN: I'm supposed to be here for two hours. I intend to see that through one way or the other and earn my wage. If you don't want to work I can't help you.

LINA: I don't want to work. I think we've established that.

DARREN: Hey, they don't pay me to be a motivational speaker.

(He studies. She draws. It is quiet.)

LINA: You know something?

DARREN: *(Zero interest.)* What?

LINA: You have a familiar face.

DARREN: You don't say.

LINA: Some people are made that way. Familiar. We always ask directions from people like that, don't we? People who remind us of . . . What? Where are you from?

DARREN: Hinsdale.

LINA: Yeah, no shit. Where in Hinsdale?

DARREN: Look, I'm trying to work.

LINA: *(Refers to her sketch.)* So am I. You're not going to tell me?

DARREN: I grew up near Willow Park, off Arbeleda Lane.

LINA: Near the big oak?

DARREN: That's right.

LINA: *(Subdued.)* They say that's the biggest tree in the county.

DARREN: *(Matches her tone.)* There was an accident there once. People got hurt. A girl. The last time I saw her . . .

LINA: She was riding her bike.

DARREN: That's right.

LINA: She was riding her bike. She was eleven. You were on your driveway playing basketball . . .

DARREN: It was getting dark. You should have been on the sidewalk.

LINA: Yeah . . .

(Silence as they remember.)

DARREN: You must feel pretty lucky having survived that mess.

LINA: So everyone keeps telling me.

DARREN: I'm sorry. It's none of my business.

LINA: That's right.

DARREN: It's just that . . . I thought that girl died.

LINA: Maybe she did.

(She hides in her sketch. Darren studies Lina with a thousand questions.)

DARREN: What are you drawing?

LINA: You.

DARREN: Can I see?

LINA: No.

DARREN: Am I inspiring you?

LINA: Look, stay or don't. Just don't talk about college anymore or class.

DARREN: Why?

LINA: Because I'm sick of the whole Q&A.

DARREN: How do you mean?

LINA: Because! You walk into Dairy Queen or something and there's a group of people in the corner you *maybe* went to high school with, and one of 'em comes bouncing up like she just found her long-lost soul mate. And more than anything in the world she wants to know, "Where do you go to school?" But she's not asking because she's interested.

DARREN: She's not?

LINA: Of course not. She asks where you go so you become obligated to ask where she goes and then, based on the answers, both parties are able to privately evaluate which of you has the brighter future.

DARREN: Jeez. Are you always this cynical?

LINA: *(Thinks about it.)* Yes.

DARREN: Well, I guess that works with the whole image you've got going on.

LINA: Excuse me? That's hardly what I was talking about and labeling me isn't the —

DARREN: Labeling you? Come on. People like you don't get labeled.

LINA: Oh, is that a fact?

DARREN: That's right. You label yourself.

LINA: Please.

DARREN: You do. You've got this whole antiestablishment thing going on so people don't have time to judge. You make the call for them the moment they set eyes —

LINA: Wow, you're about as charming as Hannibal Lechter with your little analysis over there —

DARREN: Hey, say what you want —

LINA: Thanks I think I will —

DARREN: But I know for a fact that you were a kid once and were just like everyone else and it didn't bother you one bit. You went to birthday parties, you took naps, you rode your bike down Arbeleda Lane, and you believed in things. I believe in things. But that must seem stupid to someone like you.

LINA: Yeah? What do you believe in?

DARREN: Things.

LINA: See. You don't even know what you believe in.

DARREN: Sure I do. But I'm not going to waste my energy explaining my beliefs to a cynic.

LINA: Why not?

DARREN: Because you'll just have a snappy response. It's the only reason a cynic listens.

(Something strikes a chord in Lina. Darren returns to his book.)

LINA: Do you have a girlfriend?

DARREN: What? That's none of your business.

LINA: I see. It's totally your business when you want to know who pays for my classes, but I'm out of line with a basic "yes" or "no"?

DARREN: Yes.

LINA: All right. That's fine. La-di-da-dee-da.

(New angle.)

I had a boyfriend. He treated me like shit. Isn't that amazing?

DARREN: *(Takes the bait.)* What did he do?

LINA: He had a temper. Doesn't much matter. That's just how guys are.

DARREN: Excuse me?

LINA: Oh, they start sweet as can be but after a while, they're not sweet anymore and it seems trying to make them happy is the very thing that makes them snap.

DARREN: I see. And, according to you, every guy is this way?

LINA: No, it must be me, right? I'm the stupid little girl that gets charmed into cars by greasy men holding candy.

DARREN: You're not stupid.

LINA: I know that.

DARREN: You have serious discipline problems. And you're overly sensitive. And maybe you have a few self-esteem issues —

LINA: Hey, fuck off.

DARREN: But most men are not like you say.

LINA: Yeah? Name one. And don't say "you."

DARREN: Lina, you can't believe that every guy out there is a —

LINA: Pig?

DARREN: Don't you think that most people, your average people, men shockingly included, all pretty much want the same thing?

LINA: And what, Maharaja, in your infinite wisdom, do the people want?

DARREN: I don't know.

LINA: Wow, Darren. You know? I never thought about it that way.

DARREN: *(Really ponders.)* To be free.

LINA: To be free?

DARREN: That's right. To be free. And to be loved.

LINA: *(Half serious, half teasing.)* Isn't that sweet. And that's what the people want?

DARREN: I think it is, yes. Go on, say something obnoxious.

(They stare each other down. It is Darren who looks away.)

LINA: What is this anyway? *(Snatches his book.)* *Strange Attractors and the Mechanics of Chaos.* Is this math?

DARREN: I thought you weren't interested in studying.

LINA: I'm not.

DARREN: *(Tries to grab the book.)* Well there you go.

LINA: But I absolutely must know what a Strange Attractor is . . . And who are The Mechanics of Chaos?

DARREN: They're not people. It's not a band. I don't think you'd get it.

LINA: Oh. Too confusing for me?

DARREN: I didn't say that. I barely understand it myself.

LINA: You're my tutor.

DARREN: Believe me it's nothing.

LINA: That's amazing. This whole book is about nothing.

DARREN: It has to do with motion.

LINA: Motion?

DARREN: Yeah. You know? The way things move?

LINA: And what's so confusing about that?

DARREN: You don't really want to know.

LINA: Yes I do. It sounds interesting. Seriously. What is it?

DARREN: You want to know?

LINA: I want to know.

DARREN: *(Gathers his thoughts.)* All right . . . Let us assume that . . . Everything . . . From this pen, to the grass outside, all the way up to the stars and space, everything in the universe falls into three categories of motion. OK?

LINA: OK.

DARREN: Now the first is what we call Periodic Motion, which is your basic run-of-the-mill motion that repeats itself in obvious and predictable ways.

LINA: Like?

DARREN: Like the Earth revolving around the Sun, as a really broad and bad example. We can predict that the Earth will continue to repeat the same motion, day after day, year after year, on and on until like —

LINA: Forever?

DARREN: Exactly.

LINA: Or until the Earth collides with the Sun, which is where we're headed anyway.

DARREN: *(Double takes.)* Right . . . Now, the second type would be Quasi Periodic motion.

LINA: Quasi?

DARREN: Yes. Now under —

LINA: That's a cool word.

DARREN: Yes. Now, if the Earth moves with Quasi Periodic Motion —

LINA: Quasi!

DARREN: Which it does not, but if it did —

LINA: Quasi, quasi, quasi!

DARREN: It would follow several *different* paths around the Sun and still arrive at a predetermined place. But all that is kids' stuff next to the third type of motion, which is what we call a Strange Attractor and right here is where things get tricky.

LINA: It's like a magnet right? Like two magnets coming together?

DARREN: Well, magnets that attract would fall into Equilibrium Motion.

LINA: Equilibrium?

DARREN: That's the fourth type.

LINA: You just said there were only three!

DARREN: Yes. I'm sorry I didn't mention Equilibrium. If you just understand that Equilibrium motion is nonperiodic because we know that the magnets will stop moving once they've brought themselves to each other, then you'll see how it doesn't apply. *(Lina stares at him, lost.)*

DARREN: I told you it was confusing.

LINA: Well, tell me about the strangely attractive thingy and then I think you should take a ten-minute "time out."

DARREN: All right. A strange attractor would be if the Earth were to follow one basic path around the Sun and somehow, it picks a slightly different path than it *ever* picked before. Now, because of this slight shift, the Earth will eventually take an infinite number of paths, or flight patterns, each time it orbits around. As an artist you may appreciate this. You see, if you were to draw those patterns onto your pad? If you could see the trail left behind by the orbiting Earth? You would find blossoming vistas, huge oscillating ovals, explosive and magical formations that cannot be predicted by any known measure. But, heavenly bodies are bad examples. Strange attraction deals primarily with vibrations that exist between microscopic entities, so —

LINA: So Strange Attraction is like God, then? Like, divine intervention?

DARREN: What? No. No-no-no-no-no. How do you derive — ? I explained this all wrong.

LINA: I don't think so. You're saying a strange attractor is like, justification for little tiny events we don't understand.

DARREN: Not exactly —

LINA: Why not? Take my accident. That car could have been moved by a strange attractor when it swerved off the road, right?

DARREN: It's not the same thing.

LINA: I think it is.

DARREN: But it's not, Lina. We're talking about mathematical formulae here, not the conditions surrounding day-to-day events.

LINA: Wow.

DARREN: What?

LINA: You're cute.

DARREN: What?

LINA: I said you're cute. When you smile. The way you don't get mad.

(She thinks for a moment then grabs Darren's collar.)

DARREN: Lina — ?

(She plants a kiss on lips.)

LINA: Do you want to get out of here?

DARREN: Out of here? I just —

(She kisses him more aggressively and puts his hand to her chest. They makeout. He is when he pulls away.)

DARREN: I shouldn't be doing this.

LINA: Why?

DARREN: Because I'm being paid to tutor you but instead I'm apparently working as a gigolo for the Hinsdale Community College math department! I'm breaking fifty types of honor codes here.

LINA: I shouldn't be doing this either. I just got out of something pretty bad, so . . .

(She trails off. Darren is torn.)

DARREN: Can we try again?

LINA: I don't know if we should.

DARREN: Let's try again.

(He touches her neck. They kiss sweetly then gaze at one another.)

LINA: So what about this?

DARREN: What about what?

LINA: Does this fit into your theory?

DARREN: Math doesn't apply to human behavior.

LINA: No?

DARREN: No.

(They embrace as "dreamy" music consumes the scene. Lights fade to Blackout.)

END OF PLAY

Cloudy

MICHAEL GRIFFO

Cloudy has been produced at the following places: FusionWorks'
3rdAnnual Mini-Fest, Boston, Mass; Emerging Artists
Theatre, Short Play Festival 2005, N.Y.; Playwrights' Circle
2005 National Short Play Festival, Palm Springs, Calif.;
Columbus, Ohio 2005 Fringe Festival; Offstage Theatre's
Bedroom Plays Series, Charlottesville, Va.;2005 10-Minute
Play Festival, Heartland Theatre Company, Normal, Ill.
It was also the Nominee 2005 Desert Stars One Act
Play Awards — Best Play

CHARACTERS

GEORGIA: a woman in her thirties

DAN: a man in his thirties

SETTING

Georgia's living room

• • •

Georgia, a woman in her thirties, is leaning over a table doing a jigsaw puzzle. She is standing, not sitting. She is not a woman who sits. There is a door stage left. Next to the door is a table with some things on it that we shouldn't be able to see very clearly. We hear children laughing outside, they're playing kick the can or tag, or some kid's game. Georgia loves the sound and smiles. The kids get louder.

GEORGIA: *(Good-naturedly.)* Hey I'm working in here!
(The kids quiet down, but just for a bit. Soon they are back at the same volume.)

GEORGIA: Where is the rest of the cloud?
(The kids start to get really loud, they're not having a fight, just being kids having a fun time.)

GEORGIA: OK enough is enough.
(Georgia walks to the window, we think she's going to go outside to yell at the kids. Instead she hits the off button on a tape recorder. The sound of the children stops and the room is flooded with silence. Georgia pauses a moment and doesn't move. She is thinking or trying to. Then she goes back to the table and resumes her task.)

GEORGIA: Cloud, cloud, where is the cloud? I see the lake and the trees and the pretty little duck family, but I don't see all of the cloud. Can't be a cloudy day at the lake without a cloud. *(She picks up a puzzle piece.)* Could this be the cloud?
(She tries to jam a puzzle piece into the spot without any success.)

GEORGIA: Nope. You're not the cloud, you're a . . . well, I'm not sure what you are, but you're not a cloud. Only a cloud is a cloud. Only a child is a child. Unless a child is a something else that a child isn't supposed to be.
(SFX: Loud knocking on the door.)

GEORGIA: Who could that be? Could that be the cloud? Could, cloud. Maybe the cloud rearranged itself to be a could. Could have. Would be cloudy of the cloud to do that though. Hmmm.

(SFX: More knocking.)

GEORGIA: Hold on I'm in the middle of a breakthrough. If a cloud deliberately shifted . . . out of boredom, restlessness, spontaneity to something new, dissimilar, intangible how quixotic would that cloud be? Could clouds shift? That's the question.

(SFX: Even louder knocking.)

DAN: Georgia! Unlock the door!

GEORGIA: Could a cloud have the ability, thoughtfulness, wherewithal?

DAN: Georgia! Pull yourself back and open the door!

GEORGIA: A cloud is a cloud, how could a cloud be a could?

DAN: Focus.

GEORGIA: That's Dan.

DAN: And unlock the door.

GEORGIA: Calling to me. Calling. *(Beat.)* Yes.

DAN: Georgia! That's good, you're back. Now unlock the door.

GEORGIA: Oh of course.

(Georgia goes to the door and unlocks it. She opens the door and smiles at Dan, a man in his thirties. He is wary and isn't sure what to expect from her.)

GEORGIA: Why didn't you just say so?

DAN: I . . . *(Glances at puzzle.)* I didn't want to interrupt your puzzle.

GEORGIA: Thank you for your considerateness. You do know how involved I get with the little pieces . . . so many of them, dependent on one another for their very survival . . . it's rough being a puzzle piece and *so* stressful to be a piece of the border . . . what a responsibility!

DAN: You seem . . . energized today.

GEORGIA: Oh yes. Have been . . . all day long. Well in and out. At some points this morning I felt like it was several summers ago. I'm back in the office and it's ten thirty and I've already had two cups of coffee, both large, and both with two sugars, real sugar, not candy coated imposter sugar. Real. Sugary. I'm fast-paced and in charge. I'm a piece of the border.

DAN: You're the most important piece.

GEORGIA: *(Deeply touched.)* You always say the most beautiful things to me. *(Pause.)* Why?

DAN: I don't know.

GEORGIA: You must know. You know everything.

DAN: No I don't.

GEORGIA: Yes, yes you do. That's why we all call you Dan The Man.

DAN: No, not that.

GEORGIA: Oh yes. We insist, me and the children insist that you are Dan The Man.

DAN: Well.

GEORGIA: No well. Yes, only yes. You are Dan The Man. Say it.

DAN: No.

GEORGIA: Dan please! For me.

DAN: *(Beat.)* I am Dan The Man.

GEORGIA: *(Again she is deeply moved.)* Thank you. Kindness wafts off you like perfume. Sweet perfume that you can swim in. I want to swim in your perfume Dan The Man. May I?

DAN: You really are energized today.

GEORGIA: I know! I don't know why. Oh yes I do. I don't know why I say I don't know when I know perfectly well that I know.

DAN: Why? What's charged you?

GEORGIA: The children. I heard them laughing in the garden. How they love to laugh in their little world with their little voices. Giggling, gurgling, gagging.

DAN: What?

GEORGIA: Gaggling. Not gagging. No not that. How all three of them, one by one make their voices heard.

DAN: *(Pause.)* They . . . do love to . . . be heard.

GEORGIA: Yes they do, but I love it best when they don't stand out. I love when they blend in to all the other surrounding sounds. The wind, the low-flying airplane, the chirps, when the children's sounds slip inside the other sounds a new sound is created, a soft, quiet, noise that I love so much. *(Pause.)* It's like your perfume with volume.

DAN: It is nice to hear them, isn't it?

GEORGIA: Oh yes. Do you hear them Dan The Man? Do you?

DAN: *(Beat.)* Sometimes.

GEORGIA: And I bet they're the best times right?

DAN: Yes.

GEORGIA: I won!

DAN: What?

GEORGIA: I won the bet.

DAN: Oh.

GEORGIA: I bet that the best times were when you heard the sound of the children and you said yes and that means I won. *(Pause.)* What an absolutely glorious day. I wish every day could be like this one. Quietly glorious.

DAN: Me too. Would you like anything special for dinner?

GEORGIA: Oh Dan The Man it's much too early to be thinking about dinner.

DAN: It's almost three.

GEORGIA: Three! In the afternoon?

DAN: Yes.

GEORGIA: Really? Are you sure?

DAN: Look at my watch.

(Dan extends his arm to Georgia so she can look at his watch. She doesn't just glance at it, but takes his arm with both her hands and pulls the watch close to her face so she can really see it and she keeps it there for several beats. While she's looking at the time, Dan can't take his eyes off of her. When Georgia looks at Dan, he looks away.)

GEORGIA: I'll be. It's two-fifty-seven. That qualifies as almost three. *(She notices Dan is looking away.)* You don't have to look away.

DAN: I'm sorry.

GEORGIA: Don't be.

DAN: What would you like for dinner?

GEORGIA: Not time for dinner. I know you like me. I like you too.

DAN: That's good Georgia. That makes me feel good.

GEORGIA: Like butter in the rain? Or butter in the sun?

DAN: *(Laughing.)* You're on fire today.

GEORGIA: The question is are you? In the rain or in the sun?

DAN: What's the difference where the butter is?

GEORGIA: Butter can't compete with the sun. It melts and loses. Ultimately, there is no connection between the sun and butter. But butter in the rain . . . well, the rain falls on the butter, but doesn't destroy it. It clings to it, hopefully, ever so desperately, and even if it slips off a little the butter still remains solid and strong so it can keep the rain alive. What kind of butter are you Dan The Man?

DAN: Butter that's been left in the rain.

GEORGIA: Good. I like my butter strong. It makes me feel safe.

DAN: You sound strong today Georgie.

GEORGIA: *(Upset.)* My name's Georgia, not Georgie.

DAN: I know. May I call you Georgie?

GEORGIA: Yes. You have my permission. I give it to you.

DAN: Thank you. Georgie.

GEORGIA: That does sound stronger than Georgia. Georgia's breezy, ungrabbable.

DAN: But sometimes you can grab onto a finger.

GEORGIA: Just one finger?

DAN: Sometimes a whole hand.

GEORGIA: Two hands intertwined. That's strongest. Hold my hand Dan The Man. Make me strong.

DAN: Are you sure?

GEORGIA: Yes. I want to be touched today.

(Georgia puts up her hands like she's being held up by a gunman. Tentatively, Dan approaches her and puts up his hands to mirror hers. This is very intimate for Dan and he is afraid of moving too quickly or too slowly or doing anything that will upset Georgia and ruin the moment. Dan lets his hands touch hers very timidly and waits for Georgia's response. She smiles at him, fully. Dan presses harder on her hands and then intertwines his fingers with hers until their fingers are bent and pressing on each other.)

GEORGIA: We're holding hands Dan The Man.

DAN: Yes we are.

(The tenseness and awkwardness start to dissipate and Georgia and Dan become more relaxed, they are like lovers holding hands, very casual and ordinary.)

GEORGIA: This is something we used to do isn't it?

DAN: Yes it is.

GEORGIA: You miss it?

DAN: Yes.

GEORGIA: I wish you didn't look so sad Dan The Man.

DAN: I'm not sad.

GEORGIA: You're happy-sad. Like a happy-sad pie. Your crust is happy, but your filling is sad. I made your filling didn't I?

DAN: Georgie don't.

GEORGIA: No, it's true isn't it. *(Pause.)* Please tell me Dan, the shadows don't stay away forever.

DAN: Yes, you made my filling.

GEORGIA: And yet you still come see me, and hold my hands.

DAN: And help you with your puzzle.

GEORGIA: Even though I'm sad-happy.

DAN: No, you're my Georgie.

GEORGIA: My crust is sad and my filling is happy. You're my filling.

DAN: Yes baby I'm your filling.

GEORGIA: But my crust is so thick and my filling is tucked far away isn't it?

DAN: It's temporary, it's not forever, it's not the way it always used to be.

GEORGIA: Just the way it is.

DAN: Yes, but this isn't going to be always.

(Georgia is starting to back away from Dan, she's losing control of the moment.)

GEORGIA: Might be. You *don't* know everything.

DAN: I know what you were and what you can be.

GEORGIA: Don't forget who I am. Now. Sad crust, sad, thick crust. *(Beat.)* I want to hear the children.

DAN: No.

GEORGIA: Please! Dan The Man, let me.

DAN: Not yet. Hold off just a bit. Come back.

(Georgia walks to Dan and looks into his eyes.)

DAN: Can you see me?

GEORGIA: I can see your filling.

DAN: No, just me. Just see me.

GEORGIA: I do. I do see you Dan. I see everything, all at once when I look at you. I couldn't go on if I didn't see you.

DAN: I'll never leave you.

GEORGIA: I know, you're Dan The Man. The only man for me. The only man for my children. Where are the children?

DAN: No, the children aren't here.

GEORGIA: Where then? Where are they?

DAN: Focus on me Georgie, remember what you learned. Focus on something you can see.

GEORGIA: I see you. And I know you. And right now I know I'll see you tomorrow. And I know that I'll know you tomorrow. But tomorrow I'm going to ask to hear the children again too aren't I?

DAN: Probably. Definitely.

GEORGIA: I have to ask for the children. If I don't ask for them, I won't hear them.

DAN: You can hear them. I hear them without asking. All the time. I hear them laughing and giggling and saying, "Daddy I love you. I love Mommy."

GEORGIA: But you don't hear the other sounds.

DAN: Georgie don't.

GEORGIA: The last sounds. The loudest ones of all.

DAN: You did everything you could.

GEORGIA: But I'm not a cloud. I can't be a could.

DAN: It wasn't your fault.

GEORGIA: Oh if all the coulds in the world could be clouds. Do you think they could?

DAN: I don't know Georgie.

GEORGIA: I'm losing aren't I? I'm losing again. Maybe I'll win tomorrow. Wanna bet?

DAN: I want *you.*

GEORGIA: Bet me. Bet me please!

DAN: *(Resigned.)* I bet that tomorrow you'll win.

GEORGIA: Good. Now . . . tomorrow . . . will have to show up and I'll have to be there so we can see who wins the bet. Now we just have to wait until tomorrow to see.

DAN: Yes we'll wait.

GEORGIA: While we wait can we listen to the children? You know how I love to listen to the children.

DAN: Sure.

GEORGIA: Really?

DAN: Yes.

GEORGIA: You make me so happy Dan The Man.

DAN: I'm your filling.

GEORGIA: What?

DAN: Nothing.

GEORGIA: Sometimes you're so silly. You make absolutely no sense at all. I think that's why I like you so much. You're unpredictable in your predictability. I'm going to let the children laugh now.

DAN: Wait.

GEORGIA: For what?

DAN: Just wait.

(Dan stares at Georgia. She looks at him for a few beats, then waits for him to do or say something, then starts to think this is a little weird. Just before she's going to say something Dan breaks the moment.)

DAN: OK you can listen now.

GEORGIA: What was that about?

DAN: I just wanted some quiet for a moment.

GEORGIA: You see! You're unpredictable.

(Georgia turns on the tape recorder and the room is once again filled with the voices of the children. Georgia loves the sound, but for Dan it is almost unbearable.)

GEORGIA: Listen to them go on and on! When all three of them go at it at once I have to hold my ears. But it's worth it. To hear them. Now Dan. Dan The Man.

DAN: Yes?

GEORGIA: Come here and help me. Help me with my puzzle.

(Dan moves to Georgia and stands next to her in front of the puzzle. He is in no shape to help Georgia do anything so luckily she doesn't notice.)

GEORGIA: I'm on a quest Dan, a quest for a cloud. I need to finish the cloud to finish my puzzle and the pieces are just not fitting together. I'm sure you can help me, I just sense it.

(Blackout.)

END OF PLAY

5G/10B

MICHAEL GRIFFO

5G/10B has been produced in the following places: 15-Minute
Play Festival, Finalist, American Globe Theatre, N.Y.;
Ten by Ten Play Festival, The ArtsCenter, Carrboro, N.C.;
New Gate Theatre, Providence, R.I.

CHARACTERS
NUN: late twenties to early thirties
MAN: late twenties to early thirties

TIME
Present

PLACE
A deserted island somewhere in the Pacific Ocean

• • •

Darkness. Sounds: Plane flying. Explosion. Plane falling. Explosion. Plane falling. Crash. Silence. Waves. Seagulls. Light. A Man is lying on the beach. His pants are torn and he has a bloody cut on his exposed leg. He only has one shoe on. He is clutching a small flight bag that is partially open with its contents spilling out onto the beach. After a moment a Nun walks onstage. Her habit and dress are torn and she is barefoot. She doesn't have a mark on her face. She is wringing out a cloth, which has been torn from her dress. She sits next to the Man and begins to clean his wound. After a moment he stirs, but he's still out of it. The Nun continues to tend his wound. He comes around and watches the Nun for a beat, but when he realizes what she is doing, he scrambles away.

MAN: No!
NUN: Easy.
MAN: Stop.
NUN: I was careful. *(Pause.)* I saw your pills.
(The Man glances to his opened bag that he's still clutching.)
NUN: And I've done this before.
(The Nun smiles. The Man relaxes and lets her continue to clean up his wound until she ties the cloth around it. The Man looks away from her and surveys the area.)
NUN: Does it hurt?
MAN: No. Yes. No more than everything else. *(Beat.)* You?
NUN: Quite a bit.
MAN: How long was I out?
NUN: Better part of a day. At least I think so. My watch isn't waterproof.
MAN: How long have we been here?
NUN: Don't know. I woke up during the night.

(The Man looks around the beach.)

MAN: Is there anyone else?

NUN: No.

MAN: There has to be.

(The Man tries to get up, but he can't stand on his leg and falls down.)

NUN: We're the only ones.

MAN: How can you be sure?

NUN: I've checked the whole island.

MAN: *(Incredulous.)* The entire island?

NUN: You can see the other side just beyond those trees. Our paradise isn't very big.

MAN: *(Small.)* There's really no one else?

(The Nun shakes her head. The Man turns away and starts to cry. The Nun stares for a moment, then looks away.)

MAN: I'm sorry.

NUN: Don't be. I've had more time to adjust.

MAN: This was our honeymoon.

NUN: That's nice.

MAN: There were more of you weren't there?

NUN: Five. We're hard to miss alone, impossible in a group. Would you like to pray for him?

MAN: No. Carl didn't believe in prayer. I'm sorry.

NUN: Don't apologize.

MAN: It's just that since he got sick . . .

NUN: Why waste time on prayer?

MAN: No. He prefers . . . to live instead of praying for life.

NUN: I believe living itself is a form of prayer. *(Beat.)* Do you?

MAN: What?

NUN: Want to pray.

MAN: *(Beat.)* I prayed . . . just before. And look what good that did.

NUN: *(She looks at the Man.)* I am looking.

MAN: All Carl talked about was Hawaii. I wanted to go to Greece, but he said Europe is too dangerous.

NUN: The world is too dangerous.

MAN: That doesn't sound hopeful coming from a nun.

NUN: It was quick. But slow, don't you think?

MAN: Sounded like a bomb. Do you think it was terrorism?

NUN: Why do you assume it was a bomb?

MAN: It was an explosion. On a plane. The country's on red alert.

NUN: Orange.

MAN: What?

NUN: Orange alert. Almost red, but not.

MAN: Such pretty colors forced to indicate such terrible things. The alert should be black, or charcoal gray.

NUN: That might actually make people alert. It probably was a bomb. Airplane malfunctions are much less common.

MAN: Do you remember anyone acting suspicious?

NUN: No. I was reading for most of the flight.

MAN: The bible?

NUN: No. *(Beat.)* I was reading until the first one interrupted.

MAN: What were you reading?

NUN: A letter. I suppose it could have been terrorism. How many explosions did you count?

MAN: At least two.

NUN: I thought there might have been three.

MAN: Might have been.

NUN: Last thing I remember was a man screaming. He fell on top of me and his face was inches from mine. I could smell the Bloody Mary mix. And he kept screaming, "We're all going to die." "We're all going to die!" I couldn't help but smile 'cause I've known we were all going to die since first grade.

MAN: Last thing I saw was Carl. He looked scared, but he was trying to hide it. He does that.

NUN: Then that means the last thing he saw was you. What did you look like?

MAN: Terrified. But I tried to tell him how much I love him with my eyes. I probably looked like some maniacal silent film star. Rudolph Valentino searching for the perfect expression.

NUN: Maybe you made him laugh.

(The Nun smiles at the Man. He tries to smile back, but can't.)

NUN: I love the sound of the ocean. Listen.

MAN: Who was the letter from?

NUN: Listen. Such a careless sound.

MAN: How did we survive this?

NUN: Notice you didn't ask why.

MAN: I'm trying to start small.

NUN: We picked good seats.

MAN: It can't be that arbitrary.

NUN: Why not? Actually I didn't pick my seats, Sister Eugenia did. Oh no she didn't, she was going to, but she left it up to the check-in people so she couldn't be accused of favoritism. I guess I need to thank the check-in people.

MAN: Carl picked our seats. I was in 10B. He liked to take care of all those little details.

NUN: And you let him.

MAN: Yeah, I did. I knew he really liked doing it. For both of us.

NUN: I was in 5G.

MAN: Yes, I saw you. The first row in coach.

NUN: Most leg room on the plane. Including first class.

MAN: Can you help me up? I'd like to see if I can stand.

NUN: Are you sure? It hasn't been that long.

MAN: I'm not the sit-still type.

NUN: OK.

(The Nun gets behind the Man and puts her arms underneath his armpits. She tries to hoist him up as he puts his weight on his good leg. He falls back. He tries again and gets a bit further and falls onto his good knee.)

NUN: Don't push yourself.

MAN: I'm halfway there.

(The Man leans on the Nun's shoulder and finally gets into a standing position. He's exhausted and leans on the Nun for support. His head dangling in front of him and almost resting on her forehead. After a moment he realizes how close he is to her and pulls back.)

MAN: Sorry.

(He's a bit unsteady, but he can stand on his own as long as he puts most of his weight on his good leg.)

NUN: Are you hungry?

MAN: No.

NUN: Thirsty?

MAN: I should be, but no. Who was the letter from?

(The Nun smiles.)

MAN: That you were reading?

NUN: Me.

MAN: You sat right down and wrote yourself a letter?

NUN: The day before I entered the convent. Twenty-five years ago.

MAN: And it just got delivered?

NUN: No. I read it from time to time.

MAN: Why?

NUN: It's a reminder. Of my conviction. Look at that ocean. It's gorgeous.

MAN: It's a cemetery.

(The Nun sits on the beach and leans back, digging her hands into the sand behind her. She looks up at the sun almost like a sunbather.)

NUN: A plane is so imposing above the water, so inconsequential below.

MAN: Amazing. We crashed out there. Way out there and look at us, we're alive. In tact, basically. All this time . . .

NUN: Yes?

MAN: All this time I thought I would die from . . . this. From what's inside me?

NUN: You don't like to say AIDS?

MAN: It was Carl's thing. Keep it silent, keep it at bay. I never thought I'd survive long enough to die in a plane crash.

NUN: You hardly died.

MAN: From a plane crash, sorry.

NUN: We can be rescued. It's been less than a day.

MAN: I'm not really into miracles.

NUN: No miracles, no prayer?

MAN: No offense.

NUN: None taken. For the record. I don't pray every second of the day because I believe some prayer needs to take the form of action. And I don't believe in miracles per se, but I do believe in the power of compassion. And luck, of course. We sat in the right seats.

(SFX: The MAN's watch alarm goes off.)

NUN: Someone has a more expensive watch than I do?

MAN: Carl gave it to me for my birthday last November. It came with three different leather bands, sunset, sky, and dirt. Which to straight people translates to orange, blue, and brown.

NUN: Can you take your meds without water?

MAN: I don't think it matters if I take them or not.

NUN: It does if you want to stay asymptomatic. Is your mouth too dry to create saliva?

MAN: I only have a four-day supply. The rest are in my luggage. Out there in that beautiful, gorgeous ocean you love so much.

NUN: It's elegant. Someone may come.

MAN: I thought you said you didn't believe in miracles.

NUN: This has nothing to do with miracles. Odds are someone may come.

MAN: Is your name Sister Pollyanna?

NUN: No, Sister Christopher.

MAN: That's sweet. I'm Douglas.

NUN: Hello Douglas.

MAN: Hello Sister Christopher. Kind of long though don't you think?

NUN: Some of my students called me Sis Chris. You can if you like.

MAN: What's your maiden name?

NUN: I was never married.

MAN: I'm sorry I mean your real name, your birth name.

NUN: *(Pause.)* Tiffany.

MAN: Really?

NUN: Tiffany Desirée Saint Baptiste.

MAN: Seriously?

NUN: Why do you think I changed my name to Sister Christopher?

MAN: Well, Tiffany . . . you sound like . . . well you know what you sound like.

NUN: A French whore? A misunderstood southern belle?

MAN: A very desperate drag queen.

NUN: No more desperate than a young girl from Vermont surrounded by a sea of Jennifer's and Mary Ann's.

MAN: You don't seem the desperate type.

NUN: I was. Until I received my calling from God.

MAN: I think Carl was my god. I don't mean that disrespectfully.

NUN: He doesn't take it that way.

MAN: I loved him. *(Beat.)* God, I'm already using the past tense. *(He shifts his weight.)* Oww.

NUN: Are you OK?

MAN: I think I need to sit still.

NUN: Let me help.

(Sister Christopher puts Douglas' arm around her neck and gently helps him to sit on the sand.)

MAN: You're sturdy for a nun.

NUN: You're quite filled with preconceived notions.

MAN: Sorry. I guess when the world looks at you with one big collective pre-conceived notion you start to look back at it the same way.

NUN: Two wrongs don't make a right.

MAN: Catholic wisdom?

NUN: Old Chinese proverb. We've been known to steal an idea or two.

MAN: Do you think He's watching us?

NUN: Because *I'm* here?

MAN: No, no just 'cause we're . . . His.

NUN: Would that make you feel better if He was watching us? Because He was probably watching before and it didn't make a difference to the others.

MAN: Maybe it did. Maybe they're the lucky ones. You know, they got it over quickly.

NUN: Don't be afraid.

MAN: Hard to manage my emotions at this point.

NUN: We need this time.

MAN: To panic?

NUN: To watch this magnificent ocean.

MAN: I've seen the ocean.

NUN: Not from this angle.

(The Man looks at the ocean, then grows restless and starts to look around at the sky, the trees.)

NUN: It's something isn't it?

(The Man looks back at the ocean, but this time really looks at it. He isn't smiling like the Nun, but he is growing more content just staring at the ocean and soon the urge to look away fades. They both keep staring, their smiles growing, as the lights begin to fade and the sound of the waves grows louder. The sound isn't rough, but gentle and soothing as we fade to Blackout.)

END OF PLAY

The Record

DEBORAH ZOE LAUFER

CHARACTERS

JIM: actor in his twenties
JEN: his wife, a medical student in her twenties

SETTING

A park bench in New York City

• • •

Jim stands on one leg on a chair. He simply stands, with purpose, doing nothing else. His shirt and pants are saturated with corporate logos à la racing cars. NIKE, JUST DO IT, across his chest. STP on his arm. Maybe VIAGRA or some drug company on his leg. There is a bench nearby. Jen enters with two sandwich bags. She carries an umbrella.

JEN: Hi Hon.

JIM: Oh! Hi! Did you see me last night?

JEN: Yeah.

JIM: On Fox?

JEN: All the first years watched.

JIM: How was it? Did I look OK? That goofy losing-my-balance thing — that was their idea. I was like, come on guys, this is going to be so hokey, but what can you do, right? You know these reporters. How was it? Did it look totally ridiculous?

JEN: It was good.

JIM: Yeah? Did my mom call? Did they see it?

JEN: Everyone saw it.

JIM: Yeah? Marty?

JEN: Everyone. Everyone saw it.

JIM: What did they think?

JEN: They all thought it was good.

JIM: Is that what they said? What did they say? What did Marty say?

JEN: Marty said you were a real cutup.

JIM: *(Delighted.)* A cutup? Marty said that?

JEN: Yup.

JIM: Wow! Did anyone else from the agency see it? Did they call?

JEN: Not yet. Here, I brought you ham and cheese.

JIM: Great. Thanks. It's not quite twelve yet, so . . . I think I'll wait.

JEN: Oh. Right.

JIM: People usually show up around noon to, you know . . . watch.

JEN: Feeding time.

JIM: Jenny.

JEN: Sorry.

(She sits on the bench.)

You don't mind if I start, do you?

JIM: No, no! Go ahead.

JEN: It's not like anyone's gonna to show up to watch me eat.

JIM: True.

(She unwraps her sandwich and begins eating.)

JIM: Tonight Donna Karger from New York 1 is coming again. Could you tape it for my mom?

JEN: Jim, they'll all be here tomorrow. You want me to tape New York 1 when NBC and CBS and . . .

JIM: No, tape it. Tape it. She interviewed me the first day, remember? It was great. She's really great. Tape it, OK?

JEN: OK.

JIM: Thanks. Thanks, hon. You're the best. I mean, really. I really couldn't do this without you. You know?

JEN: Yeah.

JIM: I mean any of this. Really. You're my rock, Jen. You know? I mean, behind every great man and all that.

JEN: *(This makes her smile.)* It's OK, Honey.

JIM: OK.

(There's an uncomfortable pause while she eats.)

So! So . . . how was your morning? How's the cadaver?

JEN: Oh my God. He's so amazing, Jim.

JIM: Yeah?

JEN: We separated the skin from the fascia, cut through to the trapezius muscles. It's all right there. There it is in the book, there it is on the body.

JIM: Great.

JEN: We were a little freaked out at first — Paul had to make the first cut, and that was definitely the worst, but . . .

JIM: Oh, hon, could you just scratch right back here, between the shoulder blades. It's making me crazy.

(She does.)

JEN: But it's so incredible. The human body is . . .

JIM: A little lower. That's great. Right there.

JEN: . . . with all its imperfections, malfunctions, hard-to-cut-through layers of fat, it's just so beautiful.

JIM: I can smell the formaldehyde.

JEN: *(A little insulted.)* Oh. Sorry.

JIM: Guess it's hard to wash that stuff off. *(Noticing the small crowd gathering.)* Oh look. Here come a few early birds.

JEN: How're you doing? Are you cold?

JIM: Nope.

JEN: Tired?

JIM: I'm feeling great. Top form.

JEN: It's supposed to rain later.

JIM: Crap.

JEN: I brought the umbrella.

JIM: Thanks. Thanks hon. You're the best.

JEN: Sure.

(Jim smiles and waves to the arriving people.)

JEN: *(Sighs.)* Listen, Honey. I went to see that apartment in Brooklyn again. It would be such an easier commute for me to the hospital, and you can pop in for auditions. It's really not that far.

JIM: Let's hold off.

JEN: It might not be there if we wait.

JIM: Just, don't do anything yet. Wait till you see the news tomorrow.

JEN: Why?

JIM: Just wait.

JEN: Why?

JIM: No. I'm going to announce it on air. I want it to be a surprise.

JEN: *(Very firmly.)* I think you'd better tell me, Jim.

JIM: Oh, all right. Hang onto your hat, Jen.

JEN: OK.

JIM: I'm going to try something totally outrageous and daring.

JEN: Yeah?

JIM: Something nobody will ever top.

JEN: Yeah?

JIM: I've decided to go past the record

JEN: You've gone past the record.

JIM: No, but I mean, *really* go past the record.

JEN: Tomorrow is 100 days. You've really *gone* past the record. You've topped it by two months. Nobody is ever going to stand one-legged on a chair longer. You've passed the record, Jim, and tomorrow you go in the record books, and we go back to our normal lives. That's it!

JIM: I don't want to go back to our normal lives.

JEN: What?

JIM: I want to do something extraordinary. I'm going to set a record no one will ever attempt to beat. I'll be in the record books for all eternity. I'm going to try for 100 weeks.

JEN: 100 weeks??? That's . . . that's almost two years!

JIM: Amazing, right?

JEN: It's nuts. What are you thinking? I mean, you've been out here three months.

JIM: Three months and nine days.

JEN: You're going to do this for two years? What are you going to do in the winter? You're going to stand out here on one leg all night in the freezing cold?

JIM: I think I can do this, honey. I really think I can.

JEN: What if you *can?* Why would you? What are you going to decide next? 100 *months?* 100 *years?*

JIM: Well, I'm not ruling anything out, but . . .

JEN: Oh my God. Oh my God, Jim. What are you doing?

JIM: I'm doing something nobody's ever done before.

JEN: Maybe nobody's ever done it before because it's stupid.

JIM: How can you say that? I'm inspiring thousands of people. You've seen the letters. I'm inspiring them. To follow their dreams. Their hearts. To attempt the impossible.

JEN: Oh my God.

JIM: I'm making magic.

JEN: Oh my God.

JIM: Look, Jen. You knew what it would be like, married to an artist. It's a long haul. This life. The creative life. It's a long haul with no assurances of success. But we do it because we have to do it. Because we were born to do it. It's who I am.

JEN: This is who you are. A one-legged chair stander.

JIM: And I'm finally my own boss, Jen. When I think of all the years I spent going to auditions, waiting for someone to allow me to work. To do what I do.

JEN: Jim. Honey. Is this what you do? I mean, gosh, when we met . . . When I saw you onstage . . . Your Hamlet was so exquisite. There was so much passion and depth and . . .

JIM: I got two-fifty a week for that. Maybe forty people a night saw me. Now I'm on national television.

JEN: Your Biff broke my heart.

JIM: Scripted entertainment is over, Jen. It's all about reality now.

JEN: Reality. This is reality.

JIM: I really think you could be a little more supportive.

JEN: What am I going to tell my mother.

JIM: I mean, I supported you through college.

JEN: What will Aunt Lyla say?

JIM: And that was waiting tables. Now I'm making good money. And when I make my announcement, I bet I can double the endorsements.

JEN: There's no more room on you. You're covered.

JIM: I can hold balloons.

JEN: Oh my God.

JIM: Look I don't always understand the choices you make either, you know. You spend your time cutting up dead people. Some might call that a disgusting, crazy thing to do, but do I judge? No. Because I love you. I realize that that's what makes you happy. So I support you.

(She is silent.)

What do you want? What, do you want, Jen? You want me to quit?

JEN: Well . . . yeah.

JIM: You want me to get a 9-5 job? You want me to wear a shirt and tie like everyone else? Like your father? Is that what you want? You want me to be like everyone else?

JEN: There's a big difference between *this* and everybody else.

JIM: *(Over her.)* Because if that's what you want, you might as well get a gun and shoot me right down. Get a knife. Stab me in the heart. Because that's what you're doing asking me to quit. That's what you're doing right now. *(He is gesticulating dramatically as he speaks and starts to wobble. There is a gasp from the crowd as he struggles to regain his balance. At last he does. There is mild applause. He acknowledges it.)*

JEN: I didn't think this is how we'd be spending our first years of marriage.

JIM: I know.

JEN: I miss you.

JIM: I know. I miss you too, hon. But isn't it wonderful that we're both busy? Both doing what we love? *(There is a murmur as more people converge.)* There's a pretty good crowd, now. I think I'll take that sandwich. *(She pauses for a moment. Then unwraps the sandwich and hands it to him. He begins to eat. A murmur of appreciation from the crowd. He acknowledges it. It begins to rain.)* Oh, shit. It's starting to rain. *(She regards him for a moment. Sighs. She gets up, pulls the bench closer to him and gets on it. She opens the umbrella and holds it protectively over both of them. The sounds of people gathering and rain falling merge. They stand together under the umbrella as the lights fade to black.)*

END OF PLAY

Boxes

WENDY MACLEOD

CHARACTERS

MAN: a Visiting Assistant Interim Instructor, late twenties/early thirties, new here

WOMAN: Assistant to the Assistant Associate Adjunct Provost, officious, anywhere from twenty-five to sixty-five

SETTING

The office of the Assistant Associate Adjunct Provost. College building.

. . .

An officious-looking Woman sits behind a desk surrounded by boxes of various sizes, marked with generic office categories like: DIRECTIVES, REQUESTS, REQUISITIONS, REIMBURSEMENTS. One box has no label. Man enters, carrying a large manila envelope.

WOMAN: Yes?

MAN: I'm here to turn in my forms . . . ?

(The Man hands her the envelope he carries. She pulls out a sample form, glances at it and puts it back. She hands the envelope back.)

WOMAN: *(Continued.)* You can't turn these in yet.

MAN: But we got a directive about turning in our forms . . .

WOMAN: You're early.

MAN: But the directive said sometime before the end of the semester . . .

(Woman puts her hands in a box marked "DIRECTIVES," pulls out a sheet and reads it to him.)

WOMAN: You're supposed to have a student "administer and collect the forms *shortly before* the end of the semester."

MAN: I jumped the gun then?

WOMAN: You did.

MAN: Well, since the students have already filled them in I might as well leave them off . . .

WOMAN: You can't turn them in now! We haven't got a box!

MAN: A box?

WOMAN: A box! A box! To put them in!

MAN: What about that box?

WOMAN: That box is for Directives.

MAN: And this box . . . ?

WOMAN: Requisitions.

MAN: Have you got any empty boxes?

WOMAN: Do you *see* any empty boxes?

MAN: Is that a box?

WOMAN: That box is being used.

MAN: It hasn't got a label!

WOMAN: That box is designated!

MAN: Perhaps you could double up on a box . . .

WOMAN: Perhaps you could let me run my office as I see fit!

MAN: Of course! I didn't mean to . . .

WOMAN: The number of forms we get in here, if we started putting multiple forms in a single box, well you can imagine . . .

MAN: I just thought maybe we could *start* a box . . .

WOMAN: Well we can't!

MAN: Well when you do start a box would you be so kind as to put my forms in it? If I could just set them here *temporarily* . . .
(Man tries to set his envelope on her desk.)

WOMAN: You can't leave those here!

MAN: You want me to take them away and then bring them back . . . ?

WOMAN: *Shortly before* the end of the semester.

MAN: But the directive said we have to turn them in within twenty-four hours of administering the form!

WOMAN: You should have thought of that before you went off half-cocked! Distributing forms like so many strip joint flyers!

Undermining the policies of this fine institution . . .

MAN: That certainly wasn't my intention . . .

WOMAN: Perhaps you thought you could pull a fast one, have the students fill out the forms half way through the semester, during the honeymoon period, before they've had a chance to sour on you, before they've failed an exam, been denied an extension, read the sarcastic comment in the margin . . .

MAN: *(Madly defending himself.)* We had some time, I remembered the directive, I distributed the forms . . . !

WOMAN: *You* distributed the forms . . . ?

MAN: No! A *student* distributed the forms!

WOMAN: Who collected the forms?

MAN: She did!

WOMAN: *She?*

MAN: It wasn't like that! She's very plain!

WOMAN: You didn't coax her into giving you a little peek? To get the lay of the land? To see which way the wind blows?

MAN: I followed the instructions to the letter! My hands never touched these forms!

WOMAN: But your hands *have* touched the envelope which holds these forms, haven't they?!

MAN: Isn't that allowed?

WOMAN: Assuming they don't get lost or misplaced or misfiled, the Assistant Associate Adjunct Provost will decide your future based on the forms you now hold in your hand . . .

MAN: I have nothing to fear! I'm on fire in the classroom! They follow me from course to course like so many ducklings!

WOMAN: But this early in this semester the students are undecided, they're nostalgic for the Mr. Chips they had *last* semester, they haven't *warmed* to you . . . in which case recession looms, poets are plentiful, academics adrift on the job market like so much flotsam and jetsam . . .

MAN: I was just trying to do my job! To follow the directive! A directive that wasn't, if I may say so, crystal clear!

WOMAN: Perhaps you'd like to speak to the Assistant Associate Adjunct Provost directly. He's always anxious to hear the complaints of nontenured Visiting Assistant Interim Instructors!

MAN: I certainly don't want to bother the Assistant Associate Adjunct Provost . . .

WOMAN: And yet it's his policies that you insist on questioning!

MAN: The form policy is an excellent policy but there does seem to be some confusion about the . . .

(She picks up the phone and presses the intercom button to the provost's office, threatening to make the call. Beat. The Man leans in.)

MAN: *(Continued.)* Why *don't* you call in the Assistant Associate Adjunct Provost? I think he'd be very interested to know that you *don't have a box!* (She hangs up the phone. He offers her the envelope. She snatches it from his hands bitterly. He waits. She drops it into the box without a label. He smiles in triumph, turns on his heels, and walks out. She angrily scribbles a label and slaps it on the box: FORMS TURNED IN TOO EARLY.)*

END OF PLAY

Decoding Fruit

MOLLY SMITH METZLER

CHARACTERS

DREW: twenty-six. Bipolar. A supervisor in a grocery store. Lives with his parents in Boston suburbs. He has a history of going off his medication. Upbeat, charming, and funny.

PAIGE: thirty-two. Drew's sister. An art historian who likes to read books, go to museums, and be quiet. Ambitious, pragmatic, uptight.

SETTING

Paige's humble studio apartment in New York City.

TIME

Today. 5:00 AM

•   •   •

At Rise: It is 5:00 in the morning. Paige enters wearing a long coat and scarf. She lint brushes one last shirt and places it in a meticulously packed suitcase. She checks her list. We hear a door buzzer. She zips her suitcase.

PAIGE: Excellent! Right on time! Let me just . . .
  (Paige gathers up stuff and starts toward the door. She stops to flick imaginary dust off her coat. She opens the door to see Drew standing there. He carries a makeshift fruit basket.)
DREW: Surprise, Paige!
  (Paige screams. She slams the door in his face. She steps back from the door and has a full out tantrum.)
DREW: *(Voice offstage.)* Paige!
PAIGE: No.
DREW: Paigerama!
PAIGE: NO! No, no, no, not now, not now.
  (Drew knocks loudly.)
DREW: *(Voice offstage.)* Paige! The Paigester.
  (Paige collects herself. Opens the door.)
PAIGE: No, Drew —
DREW: Surprise! What up, ho!
PAIGE: You cannot do this to me! I am literally out the door!
DREW: Gotta love Fung Wah bus! Boston to New York like that. Ten bones and you can reach out and touch someone —
PAIGE: At five AM? You didn't take your meds, Drew.
DREW: I took 'em.

PAIGE: Goddamit, no, you didn't. How many did you miss. Just today? Mom and Dad don't know you're on a field trip do they. Of course not. You're gonna let them wake up and find you gone. Scare the bejesus out of them. *(Drew manically touches everything in the apartment.)*

DREW: Did you just say bejesus? Wow.

PAIGE: My car is on its way. My flight to California is at seven and at noon I'm the guest — the guest, Drew — on Good Day San Francisco. Now, do they know you're here or not?

DREW: Me? Twenty-six. My travels? Not their business.

PAIGE: That's not true and you know it. Don't touch that! Just . . . leave it. *(Paige takes off her coat and elaborately rests it on the couch. Paige gets out her laptop and starts typing.)*

PAIGE: I'll get you on the next flight out. You have to go back to Boston.

DREW: But I'm here to see you. I missed you, Paige.

PAIGE: You saw me two days ago at Christmas dinner, Drew.

DREW: But I didn't hear about your book! I'm interested in . . . broken art? —

PAIGE: Baroque Architecture? No you're not. You didn't look up from your Super Station when I was telling everyon —

DREW: It's Playstation. And I feel real guilty about playing it. I bought you a fruit basket. I tied a bow on it too. For you.
(Pause.)
What?

PAIGE: That fruit is repulsive. *(Pause, hitting keys on computer.)* I just hope Mom doesn't wake up early. There's a 6:35 flight that lands at Logan. Dad'll come get you.
(Beat. Paige digs through her purse and hands Drew a credit card.)

PAIGE: Quick. Read me those numbers.

DREW: Why?

PAIGE: I don't have my contacts in! Chop Chop! Read me the credit card numbers!

DREW: Why? I just got here?

PAIGE: READ ME THE NUMBERS, DREW!

DREW: Why?
(Drew sits on her coat.)

PAIGE: Look, I'm sorry you didn't take your meds, but I have a book tour. Book. Tour. *(Seeing.)* Get off my coat!
(Paige yanks the card out of his hand and squints. Continues typing. She struggles.)

DREW: Is it Braille, Paige?

PAIGE: Oh, Mr. Funny. It's Mr. Funny Pants! Every time — every time — I am about to do something — something that's mine— here comes Mr. Funny. My senior prom? You have an episode. Graduation from college? You have an episode. My reading at Blacksmith? Episode. Episode. Episode. Not this time. Your flight confirmation number is *(She writes it down.)* XOCMMS1107.

DREW: Paige. I resent that. We're sibs. We're the cheese. I wanna hear more about this barracca art.

PAIGE: Here. Read my book. *(Handing it to him.)* We can talk about it when I am back in three weeks.

(Beat. Paige closes the laptop. She puts her coat back on and goes to the window to watch for the car.)

DREW: Paige?

PAIGE: Shh. Read.

(Beat. Drew does something funny with the book.)

DREW: Paige? I'm bored, Paige.

PAIGE: Read the back. *The New York Times* wasn't so bored.

DREW: *(Reads.)* "nine years in the writing, Paige Delisio delivers the single most comprehensive study of Bohemian and Moravian Baroque Architecture since Lenti's *Baroque Architecture and the . . .* "
(Reads silently.) So you spent nine years writing a better boring book than someone else's boring book.

PAIGE: I could say something not nice, you know.

DREW: Ooo. Like "at least I don't work in a grocery store and live at home, you big beef jerky head?"

PAIGE: Perhaps not in those exact words.

DREW: Perhaps not in those exact words.

PAIGE: Stop.

DREW: Stop.

PAIGE: *(To herself.)* Come on, car!

DREW: Come on, car!

(Beat. Paige huffs.)

DREW: Huff it out, girl. Work that shit out. Your life is really that bad. I mean, WHEN, OH WHEN, will you start doing something worthwhile so I can get out of the limelight.

PAIGE: One time. One time I was the hot topic at Christmas dinner.

DREW: The only thing they get to brag about me is that I know all the checkout codes for the fruits and veggies at Star Market.

PAIGE: And they literally brag about your fruit constantly.

(Beat. Paige waves wildly out the window.)

PAIGE: Finally! Excellent!

(Paige starts getting her stuff.)

PAIGE: Let's go! Hit the lights. Bring your fruit. It'll go bad. Or more bad, I should say.

(Drew doesn't move.)

PAIGE: Chop Chop. Andrew?

DREW: I'm not going.

PAIGE: I just spent three hundred dollars on a flight. You're most definitely going.

DREW: No. I am not going back to Boston.

PAIGE: Where do you think you're staying?

DREW: Si cosa et mi cosa.

PAIGE: Not funny. Not funny! Come on! I have to go!

DREW: Dan knows the codes at the grocery store and I left him in charge.

(Beat. Paige watches him closely.)

PAIGE: If you're here to stay then where are your bags? Where's your coat?

DREW: I pack light. Remember when Dad took us to Italy?

(Beat.)

Underpants. Toothbrush.

(Beat. She studies him. She knows.)

PAIGE: Drew. Bring me that fruit basket will you?

(Drew reaches for it with his right hand.)

PAIGE: With your other hand.

DREW: Fuck you, Paige.

PAIGE: With your left hand, Drew.

(Drew purposefully dumps the fruit basket in her direction.)

DREW: Don't bring old shit up.

PAIGE: Then show me. Why's your left hand in your pocket?

DREW: Cuz it's maxin' and relaxin' —

PAIGE: Then lemme see it Drew —

DREW: I can keep my hand in my fucking pocket if I feel like keeping my hand in my fucking pocket.

PAIGE: Fine. I'll just call Mom. One. Six. One. Seven . . .

(Paige goes to the phone and Drew intercepts and pulls his bloodied and ineptly bandaged hand out of his pocket. It's a mess.)

PAIGE: Oh . . . Andrew! Eck. Put it back in your pocket!

DREW: YOU MADE ME SHOW IT!

PAIGE: I thought you were done doing this! I didn't think it would be that disgusting, OK?

DREW: Look. It's still functional.

(Drew raises his middle finger pitifully.)

PAIGE: So, what? Now I have to be Florence Goddamn Nightingale right? What did you punch and when?

DREW: Cement.

PAIGE: Why? Why can't you be normal? What's the matter with you?

DREW: I got mad.

PAIGE: Well, I get mad sometimes! My apartment is a three-by-five cockroach den and my editor passed me off onto a nineteen-year-old intern and this city is so Goddamn lonely that most of the time I want to gouge my eyes out with a sharp object but I DON'T PUNCH THINGS. WHO DOES THAT? YOU, Drew. Then you show up here and tell me "you got mad"?

DREW: I got mad.

(Beat. Paige goes for the phone. Drew snatches it out of her hand.)

PAIGE: This is not my problem. You know I have to call Mom.

DREW: I'll stay here. I'll be quiet as a mouse. Get a job.

PAIGE: What can you do with one hand?

DREW: I know the fruit codes. I can get a job here —

PAIGE: Those codes are only good for the Star Market in Newton, Massachusetts, Drew!

(Beat. The buzzer rings for the door. Paige goes to the intercom. While she is there, Drew dumps her suitcase out and scatters the contents.)

PAIGE: Shit! *(Into the intercom.)* Yes, we're coming. Please wait. We'll be right down. *(Paige turns around.)* C'mon! Are you serious?

(She starts stuffing her clothes back into the suitcase.)

DREW: They said they'd commit me if I did it again.

PAIGE: Mom and Dad don't mean that.

DREW: One more time, they said. They said if I hurt myself one more time, I'm going you know where.

PAIGE: No, I'll call them from the airport and talk to them.

DREW: But if I could stay with you —

PAIGE: This is a job for only Mom and Dad.

DREW: You're not listening —

PAIGE: This is way over my head!

DREW: You're not listening!

PAIGE: I'm sorry but I don't do this! THIS is not what I do.

(The buzzer rings impatiently. Paige turns off the lights and opens the door.)

PAIGE: Come on, Andrew. Now.

(In the dark, Drew punches the wall with his other hand. Paige turns the light back on. She is stunned. He is slumped over.)

DREW: *(Through gritted teeth.)* Shitfuckshitfuckshitfuckshitfuckshitfuck . . .

(The buzzer rings again. One long irritating buzz.)

PAIGE: . . . Oh,Shit. Oh,fuck. Oh, shit. Oh,fuckshitfuckshitfuckshitfuck . . .
(Into intercom.) Go away. GO. AWAY.
(Beat.)
PAIGE: (To herself.) OK, here's what we're doing. Here's what we're doing. I don't
know what to do. I don't know what . . . I'll call an ambulance!
DREW: NO DOCTORS!
PAIGE: OK, OK, I'll get you some ice.
(She starts to go.)
DREW: I DON'T WANT ICE.
PAIGE: Maybe I have some bandages —
DREW: JUST STAY HERE. Stay.
(Beat. She sits with him.)
PAIGE: Does it hurt a lot?
DREW: Y . . . no.
PAIGE: You fucking idiot. I can't believe you did that.
(Drew stuffs his hand in his pocket.)
DREW: Did what? All better. I'm OK to fly!
PAIGE: To fly?
DREW: To San Francisco! You need a bodyguard. I'm buff. And handy, too.
(Joke.) You could definitely use someone to clean up after you. Look at
this place.
(Despite his condition, Drew starts to pick up. Paige gently stops him.)
DREW: There might be fruit you won't know in California. Like avocados. Four
One Five. (About rest of basket.) That's a two thirteen. Twenty nine nine.
Four eleven. Eighteen twelve.
(Beat.)
Whose gonna decode your fruit in California?
(Beat.)
DREW: I promise I won't punch things if you let me come. I'll just be Paige
Delisio's proud little brother.
PAIGE: You'd be bored on my tour, Drew. It's a dull book and I'm an appall-
ingly uncompelling speaker —
DREW: I'll lead the standing ovation.
PAIGE: You can come on my next book tour. When you're better.
DREW: You'll write another book, but I'll still be me. I'm not gonna get bet-
ter.
(Beat. Paige picks up the phone.)
PAIGE: (Into the phone.) Hi, it's Paige. I'm gonna be a few days late getting out
there. I'm really sick, the flu I think. Hit like a ton of bricks. When you
get this, call Janice at Good Day. Thanks.

DREW: Liar. You lied, Paige.

PAIGE: I didn't lie; I am feeling shitty. I could use a couple days watching movies and drinking ginger ale, maybe nursing some hands back to health.

DREW: When you say movies, do you mean those PBS specials about cathedrals?

PAIGE: I was thinking more along the lines of Van Diesel and Van Dam.

(Beat.)

And then a ride back to Boston. What do you say?

DREW: *(Excited.)* Do you think maybe Good Day'll send you a Get Well fruit basket?

PAIGE: *(Referring to Drew's basket.)* I hope not. I have this one.

DREW: But you don't like the repulsive one you got.

PAIGE: No, Drew.

(Beat.)

I love the one I got.

(Paige takes a bite of a piece of fruit.)

END OF PLAY

The Orphans

ALLISON MOORE

CHARACTERS

BEV: thirties to forties. Wears a nightshirt.

BOB: a little older than Bev. Wears a T-shirt and boxers or pajama bottoms.

SETTING

Bedroom of Bev and Bob in a small house. Present.

NOTE

A "/" appears at the point in one character's line where the other character should begin his/her next line, with the text overlapping through the end of the line.

•   •   •

Bev and Bob in a queen-sized bed. Bob is reading the sports page, Bev is eating a candy bar. They are surrounded by old newspapers, empty boxes of cookies and snacks, and boxes for electronic gadgets. There is a remote on the bed, with a TV at the end of the bed. The TV is off.

BEV: There's this picture in the paper today. On the back of the front page?

BOB: Yeah.

BEV: It's this picture of these people in China. A bunch of children, and this one man. And they're standing in the mouth of this cave in the mountains, just covered in soot, all of them, well, except for the man, he's cleaned his face, you know, for the picture. Did you see it?

BOB: No.

BEV: It's today's paper, I think, or maybe yesterday's.
(Bev starts looking around for the paper, never actually getting out of bed. Bob is jostled in the bed.)

BOB: Come on, I'm reading.

BEV: I'm just gonna find it, so you can look when you're done. I want to see what you think. Because, you know, I think I'm an informed person and then I see these pictures —

BOB: Informed?

BEV: I know it's here somewhere.
(Bev continues to look. Bob sets down his paper. He picks up a remote, tries to click on the TV. Nothing happens: It's the wrong remote.)

BOB: Where's the other remote?

BEV: I don't know.

BOB: I didn't turn it off.

BEV: It was off when I woke up.

BOB: If I turned it off, it'd be on the nightstand.

BEV: I don't know why I try to say anything, you never —

BOB: I heard, Chinese kids in a cave, what I'm talking about is the remote.

BEV: I could have sworn it was today's paper.

(Bob starts looking for the right remote, also never getting out of the bed.)

You'll see, they look like orphans. That's what I thought. There were so many of them, and just the one man. I immediately thought "These poor people. A fire must have burned down their village and killed all their parents, and now they're living in this cave." Because the man doesn't look old enough to be the father of that many children, you know, there were ten of them or something, although maybe, I mean it is hard to tell age with, with Asian people, you know?

BOB: "Asian?"

BEV: Well, I'm saying not just Chinese people, but Japanese, and Korean, you know, I was trying to use an inclusive term —

BOB: Would you at least look for it?

BEV: I don't have it.

BOB: Well it's not over here.

BEV: It was off when I woke up.

BOB: I didn't turn it off!

(Bev claps twice, the light goes out, there is a beeping.)

BOB: Well, thank you very much.

(Bob claps twice the light goes back on, more beeping.)

BEV: No, I ordered a thing for the remote.

(Bev claps again, the lights go back off, beeping.)

BOB: Would you stop?

BEV: Would you listen? It's beeping!

(Bob claps twice again, the lights return, and the beeping. Throughout this next, Bob claps the lights/beeper on and off, homing in on the remote.)

BOB: This is great. This is brilliant, Bev.

BEV: I saw it in a catalog, I thought it would help.

BOB: Now I gotta look for the Goddamn remote in the dark.

BEV: Over there somewhere.

BOB: I'm gonna have a seizure.

BEV: Wouldn't be so hard to find if you could listen.

BOB: I don't care about the people in China, Bev. They're orphans, it's very sad, / but I don't care.

BEV: I was trying to tell you something important, something about me, but you don't / want to hear it.

BOB: Because everything is about you, right.

BEV: What does that mean.

BOB: Nothing.

BEV: What does that —

BOB: It means exactly what I said. It's always about you. Everything. Ever since you lost the fucking baby / everything is always about you.

BEV: Take that back.

BOB: Like you're the only one / who lost anything.

BEV: You didn't go through it!

BOB: Every month, every fucking month when it comes, when you're not pregnant, I go / through it.

BEV: That's right and the one time after how many years of trying, the one time —

BOB: It was over a year ago!

BEV: I can't believe you would use our child / like that.

BOB: That's right, *our* child, he was *our* child, but the only one who ever *feels* / anything is you.

BEV: Our child, but I'm the one who *lost* him, I'm the one to blame —

BOB: No one is blaming you, I just want you to get over it.

BEV: I should be more like you, is that it?

BOB: Sometimes things don't work out way we want them to, Bev / and there's nothing we can do about it.

BEV: I should swallow my feelings, pretend it doesn't affect me?

BOB: We can't have a baby.

BEV: You never really wanted one.

BOB: Here we go.

BEV: Admit it. You didn't even cry.

BOB: All the trips to the doctors / doing my business in a Goddamn Dixie cup because I didn't want —

BEV: You didn't even cry, after four years of trying the one time / I get pregnant —

BOB: I never got the chance to cry because that's all you ever did. Somebody had to pay the bills.

BEV: I was grieving, which is what normal /people do.

BOB: I had to keep working to pay for the insurance, the fertility treatments.

BEV: You were relieved when I miscarried.

BOB: Yes, I was relieved, which is why I painted the nursery, / got that crib from my brother.

BEV: There are other things we could have tried.

BOB: Like what? Adoption? You want to adopt your Chinese orphans in the cave? / Is that what this is about?

BEV: I was talking about in vitro, but you don't / even give a shit

BOB: He said it was very small chance, / we already refinanced the house!

BEV: You don't even see how much I hate this, how much I hate —

BOB: Maybe if you tried doing something once in a while instead of lying in bed with a candy bar stuffed in your mouth our life wouldn't seem so bad.

BEV: I'm sorry I repulse you. I've been depressed if you haven't noticed.

BOB: Right, you're depressed, you're the sensitive one patting yourself / on the back for feeling all the time

BEV: I can't help what I feel!

BOB: And I'm the asshole because I don't congratulate myself every time I fart.

BEV: I wouldn't know if you feel or not, you never say a word to me.

BOB: *Because you don't ask.* When was the last time you actually asked me a question about me? Not about the baby, not how was work, but *me*? *(Silence. It is dark. In the heat of the argument, the lights have been left clapped off.)*

BEV: What do you . . . like to do?

BOB: Well. I . . . . You mean right now?

BEV: No. Anytime.

BOB: OK.

BEV: I mean. I don't really know. Seems like the past five years have been, this. You know, you come home, and you get your paper, and then —

BOB: Here we go.

BEV: What?

BOB: Everything turns back to you, what I'm not doing for you, how I'm neglecting you —

BEV: No —

BOB: You can't let it be about me for five seconds.

BEV: I take it back, please, I'm sorry. I take it back. Bob. I want to know. What were you going to say? *(Pause.)*

BOB: I like to canoe.

BEV: Yeah?

BOB: I haven't done it in a long time.

BEV: I remember you talking about that Boy Scout trip, with your dad?

BOB: Yeah.

BEV: It was Canada, right?

BOB: Boundary Waters.

BEV: So. Maybe we could canoe. Sometime. I've never done it before, but.

BOB: It's not hard, it's just you gotta balance.

BEV: Or you could go with, with Mike.

BOB: Yeah.

BEV: Or we could go? We could, take a trip.

BOB: Yeah. We could do that.

(Pause. Bob clicks on the TV, its light illuminating them in the bed. They are very far apart. Bob watches the TV for a moment.)

BOB: You know, a lot of people adopt babies from China now.

BEV: Yeah.

BOB: Phil was telling me. Because of. His sister's thinking about —

BEV: They weren't orphans.

BOB: Huh?

BEV: The picture in the paper I was . . . I thought they were orphans. I thought they lost their parents, I thought they were lost, and all alone. There was just the one man, and all these children. And the cave and. He was their schoolteacher.

BOB: Oh.

BEV: They lived in the cave. Their village was in the cave. That's why they were covered in soot. You know, from the fires inside. From cooking.

BOB: Man.

BEV: The schoolteacher was from there. He had grown up there, but had gotten out somehow and gone to college and came back to teach in this, this cave-village.

BOB: I didn't know there were still places like that in China.

BEV: They're so isolated, they speak a totally different dialect. They wouldn't even be able to understand Cantonese or whatever. They've never seen a car, because there are no roads. You have to hike for miles to get there. They weren't —. I thought they were lost, and I was lost, and I could understand, or help, but. They weren't lost at all. It's just me.

(Bev is crying.)

I don't want to be like this. I just hurt so much sometimes. I see these things and I feel so small and useless.

BOB: I know.

BEV: I don't mean to.

(Bob kisses Bev on the side of the head, touches her gently.)

BOB: It's OK.

(Bev buries herself in Bob's chest. He holds her. When she has finished crying, She remains in his arms. They watch the television. They don't look at each other.)

BEV: Do you think a baby from China would like to canoe?

BOB: I don't know. Maybe.

(They watch.)

BEV: They interviewed the teacher from the village. He said he wished they had electricity so he could bring in a TV. He said if they had a TV he could show them that the rest of the world didn't live like they do.

BOB: I bet.

BEV: That there's a better way.

(They watch in silence for a long moment. The TV turns off.)

END OF PLAY

Bedtime Stories

BRIAN MORI

*I'd like to, finally, for the first time,
dedicate the play "To MaryAnn"*

Bedtime Stories was originally produced by the American Renegade
Theatre in North Hollywood, California. David Cox, Artistic
Director; Elizabeth Meads, Co-Artistic Director; Scott Geyer,
President. The cast was as follows: Mommy: Donna Weiss; Cecil:
Tony Mosley. Directed by Nicholas Cohn. Set Design: Elina
Katsioula. Lighting and Sound Design: Donnie Roache.
Stage Manager: Mark Brush. Other productions: in New York,
New York, at the Red Room Theatre; in Hollywood, California,
at the Attic Theatre; in Atlanta, Georgia, at the Parenthesis
Theatre Club; in New York, New York, at the Nat Horne Theatre.

CHARACTERS

MOMMY: A pretty, plump, white woman, in her mid-thirties, with long dark hair. She is wearing a white sleeveless nightgown, and possesses (when "on") a sultry, melodious speaking voice.

CECIL: A good-looking black man, also in his mid-thirties, but looking at least five years Mommy's junior. He is wearing a New York Jets jersey and a pair of cotton long johns; his feet are bare. A perpetual sleepy-eyed scowl masks a gentle and loving nature.

SETTING

New York City. Mommy and Cecil's bedroom. A king-size bed with tufted headboard Center Stage. Nightstands on both sides of the bed, each with lamp and telephone. A small refrigerator Down Left. A doorway Up Left leading to the bathroom, baby's room, etc.

TIME

Winter. Early morning.

•   •   •

In the darkness we hear:

MOMMY: *(Moaning.)* Oh, baby, it's so big . . . it's so big . . . oh, I can't *stand* it . . . I'm coming . . . I'm coming . . . I'm — *ahhhhhhhhhhhhhhhhhhhh-hhhhh* . . .
(The lights slowly come up on Mommy, sitting up in bed, talking on the telephone. Cecil is hidden under a pile of covers, sound asleep.)
(Swooning and momentarily out of breath.) Ohhhhhhh . . . that was *so nice*, Jeffrey, I can't tell you. You're such a wonderful lover . . . No, I don't think that's such a good idea, I hardly know you . . . Well, I think it's better we get to know each other on the phone first. I'm kind of shy . . .
(She curls the phone cord around one finger and watches it slowly unwind.)
You'll call me again, won't you? . . . You promise? . . . Well, I'm not gonna hang up until I hear you say "I promise."
(She smiles.)
Till next time then. You know where to find me. I'll be right here. Waiting. For you. My sweet, sweet Jeffrey . . .
(She blows a kiss into the mouthpiece, waits until Jeffrey hangs up, then hangs up herself. She feels under the covers, lifts up Cecil's lifeless arm to check the

time on his wristwatch — our first view of him — and lets go: his arm flop-
ping down like a marionette.)
All right . . . that's more like it.
(She jots a figure on a pad.)
Not bad for a couple minutes work, huh, Cecil?
(She digs around under the covers, finds a box of Mon Cheri chocolates, and
pops one into her mouth.)
(Reflectively.) Still, it's kinda sad, though, when you think about it. Don't
you think so, Cecil? Sad?
(Cecil stirs under the blanket.)
Cecil?
(Pause.) Cec . . . ?
(Mommy kicks Cecil under the covers.)
CECIL: Hah . . . ?
MOMMY: You awake?
CECIL: Wha' . . . ?
MOMMY: You awake?
CECIL: *(Grumpily coming out of it.)* I am *now.*
MOMMY: I was just saying how sad it is, and all.
CECIL: *(Rubbing his bleary eyes.)* I tell you what sad, girl. You don't let me get
some *sleep*, then you be looking at sad!
MOMMY: Just think of all the extra money coming in.
(Cecil just grunts.)
Almost got enough put aside for that Civil War chess set you wanted.
CECIL: *(Whining.)* Aw, I don't care about that now, baby. Daddy just wants to
get some shut-eye!
MOMMY: Sure you do, honey lamb. Don't mind me. Go right ahead.
(Cecil turns over on his side and tries to go back to sleep . . . but Mommy
continues to rattle on, dreamily.)
You know, sometimes I feel like I'm a psychiatrist or something. Even if
it is just pretend. Least someone's listening to 'em. Someone's out there
paying attention. Someone's telling them they're not alone in the world . . .
(Cecil buries his head in his pillow and whimpers like a hurt puppy.)
Almost like I was their mommy or their lover. Or their mommy *and* their
lover. 'Cause, see, Cecil, they tell me things. Private things. Their secret
innermost thoughts that they're too afraid or too ashamed to tell anyone
else . . .
(Cecil turns over and climbs drowsily out of bed.)
Where you going?
CECIL: I'm hungry. You mind? Now that you got me up . . .

MOMMY: Look in on baby while you're at it, will ya, darling?

CECIL: Yeah, yeah . . .

(Cecil pads off to the baby's room. Mommy pops another chocolate into her mouth. Cecil reappears and crosses to the refrigerator.)

MOMMY: How's Lucius?

CECIL: Sleeping. Only one around here make any sense.

(He opens the refrigerator door.)

Whatcha got to eat around here anyway?

MOMMY: You live here, too, you know. See for yourself.

CECIL: *(Gaping blankly inside the refrigerator.)* Just as I thought. *Nothing.* When you gonna do a *real* grocery shop?

MOMMY: Have a Mon Cheri.

CECIL: I don't want no Goddamn Mon Cheri. I want me some *protein.*

MOMMY: Quiet, or you'll wake Lucius.

CECIL: I don't care, girl. This is *bull*shit.

MOMMY: There should be some leftover spaghet in there somewheres.

CECIL: Yeah? Where? I don't see it.

MOMMY: Don't just stand there like a rag on a stick, you got to *move* things, silly.

CECIL: *(Poking about aimlessly.)* I still don't see it.

MOMMY: *(Climbing out of bed and putting on her slippers.)* I swear, Cecil, you're hopeless!

CECIL: *(Protesting.)* I *don't.*

(Mommy nudges past him to get to the refrigerator.)

MOMMY: Get away from there, I'll find it myself!

(She immediately pulls out an open plastic container of spaghetti with a fork sticking in it.)

What's this?

CECIL: *(Meekly.)* Oh.

MOMMY: *(Snapping back.)* "Oh!"

(Mommy shakes her head and lumbers back into the sack, kicking off her slippers.)

CECIL: Well, what the hell it doing behind the Miracle Whip anyway? Miracle Whip should be at the *back* of the fridge. Don't you know nothing?

MOMMY: Oh, quit your complaining and come back to bed.

CECIL: Sheeit . . .

(Cecil slams the refrigerator door and hustles back under the covers with the container of spaghetti.)

MOMMY: *(Shivering.)* It's cold in here.

CECIL: Tell me about it.

MOMMY: Can't you do something?

CECIL: Like what? Landlord don't live here, what he care?

MOMMY: I worry about the baby.

CECIL: Oh, baby all right; he got more blankets than he know what to do with.
(He makes a pitiful stab at the spaghetti with a fork.)
Oh, *man* . . .

MOMMY: What?

CECIL: You wanna worry 'bout someone worry about *me*. I can't eat this.

MOMMY: Why not?

CECIL: Got shit on it.

MOMMY: What kind of shit?

CECIL: Green shit. Lookie here.

MOMMY: Oh, all that is is just the pesto.

CECIL: The *what*-o?

MOMMY: The *pest*-o.

CECIL: Look like some kind of greeny blob from the planet Neptune, you ask me.

MOMMY: I swear, Cecil, you're about as picky as a big ol' baby.

CECIL: *(Under his breath.)* I ain't too picky about my women, though, am I?

MOMMY: What?

CECIL: *(Sorry he said it.)* Nothing . . .

MOMMY: Cecil Lee, I heard that.

CECIL: So why you say "what" for?

MOMMY: Try eating around it, it's not gonna kill you.

CECIL: *(Grunts.)* Remember to put that on my tombstone.
(He twirls the spaghetti around his fork and bravely brings it to his mouth; he hesitates, then tastes it with the tip of his tongue, making a sour face. Suddenly, the telephone on Mommy's side rings.)
Don't answer it.

MOMMY: What?

CECIL: Don't answer it. Let it ring.

MOMMY: I can't do that.

CECIL: Why not?

MOMMY: S'not polite.
(She picks up the receiver.)
(In her most seductive voice.) Hellooo . . . ?
(Cecil groans.)
Well, hi. What's *your* name? . . . Ted? . . . Well, Ted, my name is Amber . . . Well, I'm eighteen years old and I'm a sophomore in

college . . . NYU . . . You're kidding! Why, we probably pass each other in the hallways all the time . . .

Well, since you *asked*, I'm five-seven, blond, and a voluptuous 37 Double D-24-35.

CECIL: *(Muttering.)* I wish . . .

MOMMY: *(Shooting him a look.)* Why, thank you. I think I'm pretty hot myself. You know, Ted, a lot of people don't realize this, but beautiful people get lonely just like anyone else. So often I find myself sitting home, alone, on a Friday night, waiting for the phone to ring . . .

(Cecil snorts and takes another bite of spaghetti.)

Well, of course, I'm not com*plet*ely alone, if that's what you had in mind. I — I *do* have my roommate with me . . . . Oh, you like that, huh? Would you like to talk to her, too? I just *know* she'd like to talk to you. Hold on. *(She cups the receiver and whispers to Cecil.)*

Cecil . . . ?

CECIL: Uh-uh. I tole you, I ain't doing no more lesbo scenes.

MOMMY: All you gotta do is say "hi."

CECIL: Sheeit . . .

MOMMY: *(Back to the phone.)* Ted? Say hi to my beautiful blond girlfriend, Heather . . . No, Heather goes to Hunter . . . Heather? Say hi to Ted, here.

CECIL: *(Garbling, in between bites of spaghetti, without attempting to disguise his voice.)* Hey, dude, what's happening?

MOMMY: *(Quickly bringing the receiver back to her ear.)* As you can see, Heather's kind of on the bashful side. But not too bashful in bed, if you know what I mean.

(Cecil grunts.)

(With a low, raunchy laugh.) Oh, Ted . . . naughty, naughty, I don't know what I'm going to do with you, I swear . . .

CECIL: *(Mouthing, mimicking.)* "I don't know what I'm gonna do with you, I swear . . . " *(And grumbles aloud.)* Sheeit . . .

(The telephone on Cecil's side of the bed rings; Cecil picks up.)

MOMMY: Tell me something, Ted. Are you alone? . . . . you naked? . . . . That's even better. So are we. I hope you don't mind, Ted, but Heather and I like to do it *real* slow, if it's all the	CECIL: Hello? . . . . Yeah, hi. How Are you? . . . Yeah? How's your weather there? . . . . Yeah? No kidding . . . . Ah, not so good here . . . . . Yeah, I don't know, in the low teens anyway; no snow, though. Hold — hold on.

same with you . . .   *(To Mommy.)*

That's right . . .   It's for you.

MOMMY: *(Cupping the receiver.)* Who is it?

CECIL: Your momma.

MOMMY: Ma . . . ? Uh — tell her I'll be right with her.

CECIL: *(Back to phone.)* She'll be with you in a minute . . . .

MOMMY: Now lay back and close your eyes. Get comfor-≈ table. . . . Good. Now pretend Heather and I are lying right there next to you. . . . Yeah, that's right. Uh — hold on just one minute, OK, Ted? Heather wants to go get her vibrator.

CECIL: Yeah, I'm fine . . . . Yeah, working hard . . . . Uh-huh . . . Uh-huh . . . Uh-huh . . . . Yeah, baby's fine . . . . Uh-huh . . . . *(Rolling his eyes.)* Yeah, we all fine . . . Uh-huh . . .

(Mommy cups the receiver and gestures for the phone.)

CECIL: Here she is. You take care now.

(Cecil hands the receiver to Mommy, pokes at the spaghetti without enthusiasm, then sets it aside on the nightstand.)

MOMMY: *(Irritably.)* Ma? You know what time it is? . . . No, it's *not* eight o'clock. It's *two* o'clock. In the *morning* . . . No, *we're* three hours ahead, *you're* three hours behind. Why is that so hard for you to remember? Hold on. *(Cups receiver, back to Ted.)* Oh, Ted, your hot body feels so good close to mine . . . Fondle me . . . fondle me, Ted . . . feel my firm round tits against yours . . .

(Cups receiver, back to her mother.) Now what's so important you have to call me in the middle of the night? . . . Ma, you've cooked chicken before. What's the big deal? . . . Well, that's *good* it came with a thermometer; it makes it a whole lot easier to tell when it's done . . . Yeah, amazing, isn't it? What will they think of next? Hold on. *(Cups receiver, back to Ted.)* *(Mechanically.)* Oh, Ted, it's *so huge* . . . I've never seen one that *huge* before . . .

(Cups receiver, back to her mother.) Now you cook it at three-fifty or three-seventy-five, whatever it says on the package, there. Hold on. *(Cups receiver, back to Ted.)* Oh, Ted, let me get on top of you. Ahhhhh . . . oh, you feel sooo good inside. Now slide over so Heather can join in on the action, too . . . That's right . . .

(Cups receiver, back to her mother.) Ma, you plan on stuffing the chicken,

too? . . . 'Cause it usually takes longer to cook if you're stuffing it, that's why . . . OK. So then all you've got to do is baste it in its own juices every half hour or so just like any ol' chicken and wait for the thermometer thingie to pop up. You got that? . . . Hold on.

(Cups receiver, back to Ted.) Oh Tedoh Tedoh Tedoh Ted . . . you're a *horse,* Ted, you're a *stallion . . . fasterfasterfaster . . .* Oh, *Heather . . .*

(Cups receiver, back to her mother.) Ma, can I go now? I'm kind of in the middle of something . . . No, I'm not mad at you, just it's late, is all, and Cecil's got to get up early for work.

(Cecil vigorously nods his head.) Yeah, Lucius is fine. Misses his grandma.

(Cups receiver, back to Ted.) Ted, I'm . . . *ahhhhhhhhhhhhhhhh!!!*

(Cups receiver, back to her mother.) Yeah, I love you, too. Bye.

(She hands the receiver back to Cecil, who replaces the receiver. Back to Ted, panting.) Sorry, Ted, you got Heather and me so worked up I dropped the phone . . . Well, listen, call again real soon, OK? . . . Yeah, that *would* be something if we ran into each other on campus, wouldn't it? Well, bye now.

(She blows a kiss into the receiver, hangs up the phone, and heaves a big sigh.) Whew! I could have done without that!

(Baby Lucius wails, offstage.)

CECIL: *(Dully.)* Your turn; I did it last.

MOMMY: Shhh, shhh, hush now, Mommy's coming . . .

(Mommy gets out of bed, puts on her slippers, and lumbers into the other room. Cecil pokes at the spaghetti without enthusiasm and sets it aside on the nightstand. The baby's wail fades, offstage. Cecil lies back and tries to go back to sleep . . . but just as he starts to doze off, the telephone on Mommy's side of the bed rings once . . . twice . . . three times.)

CECIL: *(Snatching up the receiver.)* CAN'T YOU SEE I'M TRYING TO SLEEP?

(Cecil slams it back in its cradle.)

MOMMY: *(Offstage.)* Who was that?

CECIL: *(Guiltily.)* Wrong number.

(Mommy enters.)

What's he crying about?

MOMMY: Don't know. Bad dreams, maybe. Or maybe he's just not feeling well. I worry about him, poor thing.

CECIL: You always worrying. He all right.

MOMMY: I s'pose. *(Re the spaghetti.)* You done with this?

CECIL: Huh?

MOMMY: Want anymore?

CECIL: No . . .

MOMMY: Better put it away then; last thing we need around here are more roaches.

(She puts the spaghetti back in the refrigerator, pokes around inside a moment, frowns, then closes the door. She covers Cecil with a blanket, kicks off her slippers, and climbs back into bed. Cecil is lying on his side, facing away from her, his eyes shut, his body motionless. Mommy starts to say something, thinks better of it, then closes her mouth. She digs around the covers, finds the box of chocolates, and pokes through the empty wrappers: all gone. She closes the box, sets it on the nightstand, and stares off into the deepening darkness. Then she slides down in bed, and rolls against Cecil's backside. Cecil opens his eyes, wide, tense, very still.)

Cecil . . . ? You sleeping?

CECIL: *(Gingerly.)* I thought I might give it a try; yeah.

MOMMY: *(Disappointed.)* Oh . . .

(Pause.)

I just thought . . .

(She trails off; shrugs.)

CECIL: *(Warily.)* What . . . ?

MOMMY: *You* know . . . *(Nipping at his ear.)* Maybe you want to play a little snuggle bunny.

CECIL: *(Cupping his ear with his palm.)* Oh, sweetie cheeks, not tonight.

MOMMY: Pretty please?

CECIL: Cecil *tired.*

MOMMY: Cecil always tired when Mommy wants to do it; Mommy never tired when Cecil wants to do it.

CECIL: Even Superman need a day off sometime.

MOMMY: It's more than just a "day off" — it's been *weeks.*

CECIL: Yeah? Well, it's been weeks since I got a decent night sleep around here, ever think of that? What I gonna tell Mitch when he catches me napping on the job? "Sorry, Mitch, but I was up half the night being a lesbian!"

MOMMY: *(Pouting in a little girl's voice.)* Mommy makes everybody happy, nobody makes Mommy happy.

CECIL: Oh, stop that.

MOMMY: It's true.

CECIL: Stop it right now.

MOMMY: I can't help it; it's a fact.

(Mommy's lips tremble and she blinks back tears, as Cecil searches her face.)

CECIL: What's wrong, babe?

MOMMY: *(Looking away.)* Nothing.

CECIL: Don't tell me "nothing." It's something. Why you crying?

MOMMY: You don't love me.

CECIL: How could you say that?

(Pause.) How could you say something like that? You know that ain't true. *(Mommy half shrugs and looks away; a pause.)* You know what I think? I think them lonely mothers be getting to you, that's what I think. You know damn well I love you, girl. What you talking about?

MOMMY: I'm sorry, honey lamb. I guess I'm just being insecure. I just need to be reminded sometimes, that's all. Is that so bad? We all need to be reminded *some*times.

(She runs her finger down the small of his back.) Just hug me then . . . will you at least hug me? . . . please? . . . just hug me?

CECIL: *(Grudgingly.)* Oh, all right.

(Cecil turns around to face Mommy, and gives her a perfunctory hug.)

MOMMY: Not like that, like you *mean* it!

(Cecil snuggles closer, rubbing his face against the side of her breast.)

CECIL: How's this?

MOMMY: Better . . . *(She sighs.)* Cecil? You really love me?

CECIL: Yes, Mommy.

MOMMY: You're not just saying that?

CECIL: No, Mommy.

MOMMY: Don't let me go of me, please?

CECIL: I won't, Mommy . . .

MOMMY: Promise you'll stay with me always.

CECIL: . . . I promise . . .

MOMMY: You'll never leave?

CECIL: . . . prommmm . . .

MOMMY: I'll never leave you either, Cecil. Never ever. That's *my* promise.

(Cecil drifts off to sleep. There's a long pause. The lights begin to fade.) I don't think I ever told you this, Cecil, but it's not *just* the money. I get something out of it, too. Like I was beautiful and desirable, too. Not that you don't make me feel those things, 'cause you do, Cecil. It's just that . . . I don't know, it's hard to explain . . .

(Her voice dies away. Her eyes are shimmering. She pauses a moment before continuing, staring nowhere.) When I was a little girl, I used to call people up. Right out of the phone book. Right out of the blue. Strangers. Unseen voices. Right out of the blue. Just to talk to them . . . I know that feeling of emptiness inside.

Emptiness you just want to cry out. Into the night. Cry out. Into the
world. For something. Someone. Just to let them know you're alive . . .
(Pause.)
Cecil . . . ? Cec . . . ?
(But Cecil is sound asleep. Mommy gently strokes his head.) Sleep . . . sleep,
precious . . . sleep, my baby . . . sleep . . . sleep . . . sleep . . .
*(The phone rings on Mommy's side of the bed, but she makes no effort to
answer it. She kisses the sleeping Cecil's forehead and rubs her chin against
his head, as the lights fade slowly to black.*

END OF PLAY

The Morning After

CAREY PERLOFF

CHARACTERS

> MATT: a twenty-something graphic artist who needs his sleep
> JESSICA: Matt's high-strung girlfriend, who works for the mayor's office

TIME

> April 18, 2006, 4 AM

PLACE

> A second-story flat in the Mission District, San Francisco

• • •

A rumpled bed in a small second-story flat in a Victorian house in the Mission District of San Francisco, at 4 AM. Matt and Jessica are sleeping. An alarm goes off. Matt's hand reaches out to slam it off. Jessica sits up in bed.

JESSICA: Wait!

MATT: Sssshhhhh . . . *(He rolls back over, asleep.)*

JESSICA: Was that the alarm?

MATT: *(Muffled.)* It was a mistake — it's four AM.

JESSICA: I *know* it's four AM — I *set* it for four AM!

MATT: You're *nuts*—

JESSICA: Wake *up!* Wake up and smell the coffee! *(She throws off the blankets.)*

MATT: What coffee? It's *freezing* — stop it —

JESSICA: We have to get *moving* —

MATT: *(Grabbing the blankets.)* Jessica! It's the middle of the *night!* Even the *drug dealers* are asleep. What are you *doing?*

JESSICA: It's a surprise! *(She starts grabbing clothes off the bureau.)* Here! Quick! Your suit!

MATT: *What* suit!

JESSICA: I borrowed a suit! From Brian. It's Monday — the restaurant is closed —

MATT: Am I missing something here?

JESSICA: Today today today! What is *today?*

MATT: It's not *today* — it's *tonight* — I'm *sleeping* — go *away* —

JESSICA: *Think!* Think, Matt! April 18! What happened on April 18?

MATT: Napoleon invaded Russia. Go to *sleep.*

JESSICA: He *did?*

MATT: What?

JESSICA: Napoleon invaded *Russia* on April 18?

MATT: How the hell do I know what day Napoleon invaded Russia!

JESSICA: That's an incredible coincidence!

MATT: If you don't turn off the light and leave me *alone* —

(Jessica goes to the foot of the bed, lifts it with difficulty, and starts shaking it violently.)

MATT: Jesus Christ — what is the —

JESSICA: Feel that? What's it feel like, Matt? Close your eyes and imagine! *(She shakes the bed harder, throws pillows around, etc. Mock cries.)* Help! Help! What's happening? Oh God! The ground is shaking beneath my feet —

MATT: *(Mocking her.)* What's happening? Oh God! My girlfriend is losing her mind! *(Throws pillow at her.)* STOP IT! I MEAN IT! What is the *matter* with —

JESSICA: It's an *earthquake*, idiot! The Great Quake. April 18, 1906. That's a hundred years ago, *today* —

MATT: So *what*?

JESSICA: We're going to make *history*, Matt darling. *We're* going to be the ones above the fold in the *Chronicle* when people open their papers tomorrow morning —

MATT: You *hate* the *Chronicle* — you refuse to even *read* the *Chronicle* —you told me it was for intellectual *midgets* —

JESSICA: That's *irrelevant! (Trying to pull him out of bed.)* Come on! We're going to Golden Gate Park, Matt! Right now, Matt! We're going to stand under the Portals of the Past at the precise moment the earthquake happened, Matt —

MATT: No!

JESSICA: Yes!

MATT: Go by yourself!

JESSICA: I can't, you idiot! Don't you *get* it? At exactly five AM, in celebration of a hundred years of survival — you and I are going to get *married.* *(Matt sits up, stunned.)*

MATT: Say that again?

JESSICA: We're going to stand under the Portals of the Past and —

MATT: *(Interrupting.)* What the hell are the Portals of the Past?

JESSICA: You know those incredible columns in the middle of the park? — they used to be part of a mansion on Nob Hill — owned by some railroad magnate — and when the earthquake hit, the whole house crumbled except the beautiful columns by the front door — and there they sat amidst all the devastation like some fabulous Greek ruin until finally someone moved them to the Park as a memorial and I was running past them the other day and I thought — how *perfect!* It's the perfect *metaphor!*

MATT: Who said anything about getting *married?*

JESSICA: We have to do *something* to commemorate the event — it was so unbelievable — one minute the city was standing and the next it was like a pile of dominoes and two hours later the flames had devoured everything and people were living in tents in the park and —

MATT: I know! I *know!* Ever since you started working for the mayor's office you've become like the *History Channel* —

JESSICA: History is *important,* Matt! The present is just a tiny moment in a huge continuum and —

MATT: I don't *care!* I'm exhausted! My head is killing me and I refuse to put on Brian's waiter suit and I certainly have no intention of getting *married!* Where do you come *up* with this stuff?

JESSICA: We *love* each other.

MATT: I know we love each other, Jessica, but I need my *sleep!* If I don't get at least eight hours-

JESSICA: *(Interrupting.)* Don't you remember after 9/11 how suddenly everyone started getting married because they realized there might be no tomorrow —

MATT: And an equal number of people ended their relationships because they realized the same thing . . .

JESSICA: Do you want to end our relationship? Is that what you're —

MATT: No! Go *away!*

(He dives under the pillow. The alarm goes off again. Matt flails around looking for the clock.)

MATT: Jesus — this is a nightmare!

JESSICA: We've still got *time!* Fifteen minutes to shower and dress—twenty minutes to cab to the park —

MATT: And *what?* What *then?* Some priest in his jogging clothes gets pulled over to perform the —

JESSICA: No — you don't understand — we'll be one of *hundreds* — like all the gay couples on the steps of City Hall the day Newsome decided to marry them — *history,* Matt! We'll be making history!

MATT: You mean other people are doing this too?

JESSICA: Absolutely! All over the city, under cover of darkness, couples are crawling out of bed and dressing up in fancy clothes and making their way to the center of Golden Gate Park before sunrise, to be part of an incredible event —

MATT: That is so creepy — like the Moonies — how *can* you —

JESSICA: I want to be *part* of something, Matt! I never went to a *Dead* concert. My parents put me to bed before I could see *Armstrong* walk on the moon.

I was never arrested in an *antiwar* demonstration or competed in a national *spelling bee* — I never even ran Bay to Breakers!

MATT: *OK!* We'll run Bay to Breakers! Next year — I promise — we'll dress up in clown suits like the rest of San Francisco and we'll line up and — *(He stops. There is a rumble. Two books fall off the shelf.)* Oh God! What was—

(Another rumble.)

JESSICA: Did you feel that?

MATT: Come here!

JESSICA: No!

(A rumble. More books off the shelves. Crash.)

MATT: Jesus — don't tell me —

JESSICA: Oh my God —

MATT: Come here, baby. Quick. Get under the bed —

JESSICA: Why?

MATT: That's what you're supposed to do — you get under the bed —

JESSICA: I think it's stopped —

MATT: No — that was just the warning — oh God — I can't believe this is happening—come *on* —*(Grabbing her.)*

JESSICA: Leave me alone! What do *you* care?! You wouldn't even come to Golden Gate Park and get —

(A big rumble. More books crash. A mug with colored pens and rulers falls, and the pens scatter everywhere. Matt screams.)

MATT: Shit! My drafting pens! Help! *(From under the bed.)* Come *on* — get under the bed — get under the bed baby! I love you, Jessica — you know I love you — get under the —

JESSICA: Hypocrite! You want to *die* with me but you don't want to —

(A huge crashing sound.)

MATT: OK! OK! Whatever you say — get away from the *door* —

(Jessica is walking over to the window.)

No — not the window — that's worse — get *down* — !

JESSICA: *(Looking out window.)* It's *garbage* —

MATT: Be careful!!

JESSICA: It's *garbage*, you idiot!

MATT: What are you —

(Sound of garbage cans being overturned and trash being crunched outside the window — Jessica crosses away and sits on the bed.)

MATT: Garbage?

JESSICA: It's Monday. Garbage day.

MATT: *(Climbing out slowly from under the bed.)* Jesus — I thought it was —

JESSICA: I know —

(The garbage truck revs up and drives away. It is silent.)

MATT: I've never heard anything that *loud* — all my pens . . . *(Staring at the floor.)*

JESSICA: Yeah —

MATT: I guess I've never been *awake* at 4:30 in the morning before . . .

JESSICA: I guess not —

MATT: *(Climbing back in bed and reaching for Jessica.)* I'm sorry—

JESSICA: *(Resisting.)* What time is it?

MATT: Hard to say — the clock fell —

JESSICA: *(Moving away, sadly.)* I'll bet it's five —

MATT: It's freezing — come here —

JESSICA: *(With great sorrow, looking out the window.)* We missed it.

MATT: What?!

JESSICA: It's over. A bunch of lovers just made history and we missed it.

MATT: No we didn't! I mean — we *experienced* it. Right here in our own bedroom.

JESSICA: *(Depressed.)* It was *garbage* —

MATT: I *know!* But it felt like the real thing! Didn't it, baby? *(He puts his arms around her.)*

JESSICA: No, Matt. No, it didn't. *(She wails.)* What are we going to *do?*

MATT: Sleep.

JESSICA: No. Sleep is not an option.

MATT: Sex? *(He reaches toward her.)*

JESSICA: I wanted an earthquake. Or at least a mass wedding.

MATT: I know. *(He kisses her.)* Next time. *(Pause.)* I promise.

(Blackout.)

END OF PLAY

On the Edge

CRAIG POSPISIL

On the Edge was produced by the Vital Theater Company (Stephen Sunderlin, Artistic Director) in New York as part of the Vital Signs VIII on October 30, 2003. It was directed by Tom Rowan, and the cast was as follows: Gene: Rob O'Hare; Samantha: Anastasia Barnes. The play was also staged as part of the American Globe Theater and Turnip Theater Company's Seventh Annual Fifteen Minute Play Festival in April 2002 in New York. The play was directed by Tony Pennino, and the cast was: Gen: Clayton Hodges; Samantha: Rachel Jackson.

CHARACTERS
GENE: seventeen, a senior in high school, sensitive
SAMMY: seventeen, a female classmate of Gene's, seen it all

PLACE
A ledge and window on the exterior of a New York apartment building

TIME
Early fall

• • •

It is night, and Gene, a young man of seventeen, stands on a ledge on the outside of a building, ten stories up in the sky. He is plastered against the wall of the building, not moving a muscle. Every so often, he glances down to the street, and scans it, before looking up again.

Several feet away from him there is a dimly lit, open window. From inside the apartment rock music and snatches of conversation can sometimes be heard.

After a few moments, Sammy, a young woman of seventeen, appears in the window. She sticks an unlit cigarette in her mouth and pulls a match out of a matchbook. She strikes the match against the book a couple of times, but the match doesn't light. She tosses the match out the window, . . . and notices Gene.

Long pause. They look at one another.

SAMMY: Hey.
GENE: Hey.
   (Sammy glances down at the sidewalk as she tears another match out of the book and tries lighting it. Before it catches though Gene speaks up.)
GENE: Ah . . . would you mind waiting a couple minutes?
SAMMY: Huh?
GENE: Cigarette smoke really bothers me.
SAMMY: Oh. Sure.
   (Gene looks down and scans the sidewalk again. Sammy follows his gaze and then looks back at him.)
SAMMY: So, what's up? You're missing the party.
GENE: I'm just hanging out.
SAMMY: That's cool.
   (Pause.) How's the view?
GENE: I can see my building from here.

SAMMY: *(Slight pause.)* I know you. You're in my physics class, right?

GENE: Yeah.

SAMMY: What's your name?

GENE: Gene.

SAMMY: Right. Right.

GENE: You're Samantha. Sammy.

SAMMY: Yeah. How'd you know?

GENE: . . . you're in my physics class.

SAMMY: Oh. Yeah.

    (Pause.) So, what're you doing?

GENE: What does it look like I'm doing?

SAMMY: It looks like a major bid for attention.

GENE: With *my* parents? I stopped trying.

SAMMY: *(Pause.)* So, what's the deal?

GENE: *(Shrugs.)* I decided life's just not worth it.

SAMMY: Bummer.

    (Pause.) So, what're you waiting for?

GENE: Amanda.

SAMMY: Amanda Harris?

    (Gene nods. Sammy looks over her shoulder back into the apartment and then back at Gene.)

SAMMY: You want me to get her?

GENE: No, I'm waiting for her to leave.

SAMMY: But then you'll miss her.

GENE: Not by much.

SAMMY: Whoa. That's harsh.

GENE: Yeah, well, . . . so's life.

SAMMY: So, what happened? She dump you?

GENE: We weren't dating.

SAMMY: So, she wouldn't go out with you?

GENE: . . . no. Not really.

SAMMY: *(Slight pause.)* Did you ask her out?

    (Pause.) Gene?

GENE: I don't wanna talk about it.

SAMMY: Hey, I just want to be able to tell people why you did it. I mean, I'm sure to be interviewed by the news and the tabloids. After they hose you off the sidewalk.

GENE: They'll know.

SAMMY: Did you leave a note?

GENE: *(Slight pause.)* No.

SAMMY: Do you want some paper?

GENE: Would you go away?

SAMMY: If you don't leave a note, how's anyone going to know why you did it?

GENE: Because I'm gonna scream her name out as I fall, OK?!

SAMMY: *(Pause.)* What if you can't finish?

GENE: What?

SAMMY: I mean, do you have this timed out? How long will it take? Probably the sort of thing, I could figure out if I paid attention during physics. But, I mean, what if you only get to say, "Aman— !" before you hit?

GENE: I'll finish.

SAMMY: There's a breeze. What if the wind takes the sound away?

GENE: I'll make sure they hear me.

SAMMY: I'm just trying to help.

GENE: I think I can handle it.

(Pause.) You know, this isn't gonna be pretty. I'm gonna split open on the sidewalk when I hit. If I don't jump far enough, I might impale myself on that iron fencing. So, unless you wanna have nightmares about this for the rest of your life, you might wanna go.

SAMMY: No, I'm cool.

(Pause.) I don't think Amanda knows you like her so much.

GENE: I don't like her. I *love* her.

SAMMY: Whatever. You should tell her.

GENE: *(Pause.)* I can't.

SAMMY: It's gotta be easier than this.

GENE: Yeah, but this makes more of statement.

SAMMY: A statement about what?

GENE: It's just more dramatic, OK?!

SAMMY: Oh! I know where else I've seen you. You're in all the plays at school, right?

GENE: Yeah.

SAMMY: No wonder.

GENE: "No wonder" what?

SAMMY: You theater people are weird.

GENE: We are not!

SAMMY: Dude, you're on a ledge.

GENE: *(Pause.)* You don't understand.

SAMMY: Maybe not.

(Slight pause.) Does your shrink understand?

GENE: I don't go to a shrink!

SAMMY: Something to think about.

(Slight pause.) But, you know, Amanda's not so great. She's got a hot body, yeah, but she's kinda obvious. I mean, she's the sort of pretty you like to look at, but I can't imagine what I'd talk to her about.

GENE: No, she's really nice. She always smiles at me in the halls at school, and I run into her sometimes when I'm walking my dog, and we say hi, and then she talks to Molly, and pets her. She's not like you think.

(Slight pause.) I love her voice. It's kind of rough, but sweet.

SAMMY: Yeah, she's got a kinda sexy voice.

(Pause.) So, where do you live?

GENE: What?

SAMMY: I live near Amanda too. East 78th between Park and Lex. So where are you?

GENE: Why do you want to know?

SAMMY: Jeez, I'm just curious. I thought maybe we could share a cab across the park.

GENE: After I kill myself?!

SAMMY: Oh, yeah, right. I forgot.

GENE: Stick around. You'll see.

SAMMY: Uh-huh.

(Pause.) Wait a minute. You said you could see your building. This is the West Side. You don't live near Amanda.

GENE: *(Slight pause.)* I didn't say I did. I said I saw her walking my dog.

SAMMY: Oh, man.

GENE: What?

SAMMY: Tell me you don't drag your dog across town, hoping you'll run into her.

GENE: No. We just go for long walks.

SAMMY: Oh, man. You're like a stalker.

GENE: I am not.

SAMMY: Oh, wow. Now that's an angle for the tabloids. Wait 'til I tell people.

GENE: No! Don't!

(Slight pause.) Please.

SAMMY: Then come back inside and talk to her.

GENE: No. I can't.

SAMMY: Why not? I'll help you find her.

GENE: Because she's got her tongue halfway down Bobby Chamberlain's throat, OK?!!

(Pause.) I ran into her when I was walking Molly last weekend, and we talked and she said was coming to M.J.'s party tonight, and I said I was

too, and she said, "Great. I'll see you there. We can hang out." I've been waiting all week for this party. I thought, "Perfect. We'll talk a little, then I'll ask her out." I've wanted to for months, but first she was dating Dean and then Chris, but . . . . Well, I got here right at eight. I was the first one here. And I waited near the door. And I waited, and waited. And I drank a lot while I was waiting, . . . and then she came in. And Bobby had his arm around her neck.

(Pause.) So, then I had to go throw up for a while. And when I got back she was making out with him on the couch. So I then I went to throw up a little more, and as I came out of the bathroom, I saw them duck into M.J.'s mother's bedroom.

(Slight pause.) All I wanted was hold her hand and smell her hair, . . . and now she's down the hall fucking him!

(Long pause.)

SAMMY: Bobby's kinda cute, you know.

GENE: What?!

SAMMY: Well, he is.

GENE: He's an idiot. We've been going to school together for eight years and he still can't remember my name. He's always . . . I mean, it's like other people just don't . . . He's an asshole!

SAMMY: Hey, he's not my type, but a lot of girls go for him.

GENE: Oh, go away! Please?!

SAMMY: The thing is you shouldn't have waited to ask her.

GENE: Like I don't know that! Like that's not the reason I'm out here. I'm a loser. I'm weak! No one wants to be around me. I get it! I know, OK?!

(Slight pause.) I can't take it any more, all right?! I'm tired. I'm tired of trying to "just keep smiling," like my mother says. Or go, "Well, some people are late bloomers."

(Pause.) I can't.

(Long pause.)

SAMMY: Gene, ...

GENE: What?

SAMMY: I've got bad news.

GENE: You're fucked up, you know that!

SAMMY: Amanda's gone.

GENE: *(Slight pause.)* Bullshit. I'm not falling for that.

SAMMY: You must've missed her while we were talking. I bummed that cigarette from her as she and Bobby left.

GENE: No! You're lying! I've been watching. I couldn't have missed her.

SAMMY: OK, fine. Keep waiting then. I'm going back inside.

GENE: No, wait!

SAMMY: What?

GENE: You're just gonna go in there and tell people or call the cops. Or you'll tell Amanda not to leave.

SAMMY: I'm telling you, Gene, she's already gone.

GENE: I was watching.

SAMMY: Fine, she's still here. Me, I need a drink.

GENE: If you go, I'll jump.

SAMMY: Yeah, so? I thought you were gonna jump anyway.

GENE: But I'll jump now. And it'll be your fault.

SAMMY: I can live with that.

(Sammy turns and disappears into the apartment.)

GENE: Hey! Sammy? Sammy?!

(Slight pause.) Bitch!

(Sammy suddenly reappears in the window.)

SAMMY: Wha'd you call me?!

(Gene flinches and struggles to keep his balance.)

GENE: Jesus Christ! Don't do that.

SAMMY: What did you call me?

GENE: Oh, give me a break.

SAMMY: No one calls me that!

GENE: Everyone calls you that.

SAMMY: What?

GENE: Everyone calls you a bitch.

(Slight pause.) And after tonight I know why!

SAMMY: Knock it off, asshole!

GENE: Or what?

(Sammy climbs out onto the ledge and starts inching her way toward Gene.)

GENE: What the hell are you doing?!

SAMMY: I'm gonna make you shut up.

GENE: You stay away! You . . . oh, I get it. This is like reverse psychology. You say you'll push me, so I say, "No, no, I want to live."

SAMMY: No, I'm just pushing you.

GENE: I'll take you with me!

SAMMY: Like I care.

GENE: OK, OK, I'm sorry.

(Sammy stops. She is about a foot or two away from him.)

SAMMY: Whatever. Forget it.

(Slight pause.) Hey, . . . this is kinda cool out here.

(There is a pause as Gene gets his breath back.)

GENE: Oh, man, I am so fucked up.

SAMMY: You just need to talk to a shrink or something.

GENE: I don't think I could.

SAMMY: It's not so hard.

GENE: *(Slight pause.)* You go to one?

SAMMY: Yeah.

GENE: How come?

SAMMY: My parents make me go.

GENE: You're kidding. Why?

SAMMY: They're worried I'm a lesbian.

GENE: Oh, that's fucked! Why do they think that?

SAMMY: 'Cause I'm a lesbian.

GENE: *(Pause.)* What?

SAMMY: I like girls.

GENE: Really?

SAMMY: Yeah.

GENE: Whoa.

> *(Slight pause.)* What's that like?

SAMMY: I don't know. Probably like you liking girls.

GENE: Does anyone else know?

SAMMY: No.

GENE: What does your shrink say?

SAMMY: Not much.

GENE: What do you say?

SAMMY: That I don't have a problem liking girls.

GENE: Is that true?

SAMMY: Yeah. I mean, sometimes . . . no, I don't have a problem with it. My folks are kinda messed up about the idea, though. They said they'd like disown me or not pay for college or something. It's a drag.

GENE: So, what are you going to do?

SAMMY: I don't know. Try to hold out until I get through school and college and then get away or something.

GENE: That sucks.

SAMMY: I guess.

> *(They are silent for a moment.)*

GENE: My parents are nuts, but . . . not like that.

SAMMY: Good.

GENE: You wanna go back in?

SAMMY: In a minute. It's kinda fun out here.

GENE: Yeah, it's a rush when the wind blows by.

SAMMY: Yeah?

GENE: Yeah. Wait . . . here it comes.

(*They stand there feeling the breeze. The wind picks up a bit and they spread their arms flat against the wall for extra support. Their hands touch, and they laugh, surprised. They take each other's hand and wait for the next breeze. The lights fade to black.*)

END OF PLAY

2B (or Not 2B)

PART ONE

JACQUELYN REINGOLD

2B (or Not 2B) had a staged reading in "Acts of Love" a benefit for
Cure Autism Now at the Canon Theatre in Beverly Hills, on
October 20, 2003. It was directed by David Tochterman.
The cast was: Franny: Julie Warner; Dave the Bee: Patrick
Warburton. *2B (or Not 2B)* was first fully staged at the Actors
Theatre of Louisville on February 2, 2005. It was directed by
Erica Bradshaw. Sets by Brenda Ellis; costumes by Kevin Thacker;
lights by Matt Cross and Katie McCreary; props by Joe
Cunningham and Deanna Hilleman; dramaturg, JoSelle
Vanderhooft. The cast was: Franny: Anna Bollard;
Dave the Bee: Ian Frank.

CHARACTERS

FRANNY: a woman in her thirties
A BEE: a male bee named Dave

TIME

Now

PLACE

Franny's studio apartment in Upper Manhattan

• • •

Franny, upset, disheveled, in her studio apartment, on the phone, and waxing her legs. She talks fast.

FRANNY: I know you told me it was over and I respect that I mean I understand it and I know you don't want to see me again and I know I was not very nice to you — at times — and I just want to say that I've had a well a complete not-nice-ostomy and a total unlike-ectomy, I've had all the not nice unlikable parts removed so if you call me I'm sure we can work it out. *(She hangs up. She tears off a strip of wax from her legs.)* AH! *(She cries. She dials. She holds the receiver to her leg. She rips wax.)* Ah! I'm waxing my legs. I know you hated my hairy legs, so I'm waxing! I can't believe you haven't called me back. *(Hangs up. Rips off more wax.)* Ah! *(Dials.)* I heard you asked out my friend Eleanor, and I thought you'd like to know she has the papilloma virus — *in her vagina.* And in her mouth. On her tongue. In case you happened to have kissed her already. Wouldn't worry about it though, I'm sure it's fine . . . OK, well, thanks for breaking my heart. And I still really love you and if you want to change your mind and give it another try, let me know. *(Hangs up. Cries. Rips wax.)* Ah! *(A human-sized bee appears.)*
FRANNY: *(Continued.)* AHH!! *(She hides her head, she looks.)* Ohmigodohmigodohmigod! *(She tries to hide. The bee is huge. There's nowhere to go. She runs into a corner.)* Ohmigod. OK. Could you just go? Please. Um. Shoo. Go. *(He doesn't budge.)* Look, the park is a few blocks away, if you could just fly over there. I'm sure you'd be happier. *(He doesn't move. She crouches to the floor. Or hides under the bed.)* Or or in the back, there's a garden. With uh plants. Or, my neighbor, downstairs, she has these window boxes: geraniums, impatiens. I'm sure you're in the wrong place.

BEE: Is this 2B?

FRANNY: What?

BEE: 2B or not 2B?

FRANNY: It's a joke, right?

BEE: I wouldn't make a joke like that.

FRANNY: OK, this is 2B, but I'm sure it's the wrong building.

BEE: 344 West 188 Street?

FRANNY: *(She grabs her bag, and tosses it at the bee.)* OK, take whatever you want. I only have ten dollars, but I'll write down my PIN number. My bank's on the corner, you can have it all.

BEE: I don't want your money.

FRANNY: Then take the Tivo. Or or the organic honey, OK?

BEE: I don't want that.

FRANNY: Look, I'm possibly allergic. And my epipen will not be of much use in this case cause you are ohmigod so fucking big you are the biggest bee I have ever seen. I can't believe this is happening. *(She grabs the phone.)* Frank. Help! There's a giant bee in my apartment. Could you come over? Please!

BEE: He's a jerk. Forget about him.

FRANNY: What?

BEE: You deserve better.

FRANNY: Well, thank you, I will consider that. Now please, go away. Or I'll call the police.

BEE: I don't think they'll come for a bee.

FRANNY: I am really afraid of you. I mean really afraid. Bees are my well thing you know some people it's snakes or heights or whatever, but me, it's bees.

BEE: I won't hurt you.

FRANNY: Well that's nice to hear but.

BEE: Why would I hurt you?

FRANNY: I don't know. Because you're a bee.

BEE: Have you been hurt before?

FRANNY: Yes.

BEE: Yellow jackets.

FRANNY: No bee. Bees. I've been stung. So I am sure you are in the wrong apartment.

BEE: It's the right apartment.

FRANNY: Then it's the wrong species. I'm a human, a female human, and and you're not invited.

BEE: How's that going for you?

FRANNY: What?

BEE: Being a female human?

FRANNY: It's fine. It's just fine.

BEE: Work and love, it's all good? How's your job?

(Franny sneaks toward the window while talking:)

FRANNY: Fine. I'm a receptionist. It's a career change. I used to be a painter. Very cutting edge, I didn't even use paint, I used body fluids, but um it didn't work out because, several others already claimed that niche, you wouldn't believe what some people do with their menstrual blood, so now I uh have a job and a boss and uh — *(She can't get out the window.)*

BEE: And your human female love life?

(Franny crawls all around the room, heading toward a certain cabinet while talking:)

FRANNY: Well my first relationships were with typical self-involved commit-mentphobes when I was between the ages of say, five and twelve. Then junior high was alcoholics, high school was drug addicts, college: gay men, a guy who owned a duck, then a physically challenged interpretive ice skater meaning you know an amputee who'd skate with a kind of stick with a blade at the bottom, then I married a guy who liked to put garlic in his ears, but I went away a lot with my boyfriend who was a puppeteer for the blind, then my husband fell for a woman with small limbs, and I got pregnant but lost the baby and the father, well he was a mid-westerner, so, then I had a slew of Internet dates with incredibly boring men which is I guess a sign of getting older the men tell long stories that sound like intricate recipes on how to marinate poultry. *(Franny has snuck around to her cabinet, pulled out a can of bug spray, and points it at the bee.)* OK. Get out. Or I will spray you with this deadly spray. *(She sprays. The can is empty. She shakes, tries again, nothing.)* Damn. *(She runs for the door. It won't open.)*

BEE: You like flowers, don't you, Franny?

FRANNY: How do you know my name?

BEE: *(Pulls out a bouquet.)* And tulips are your favorite, aren't they?

FRANNY: How do you — ? OK. Thanks for the delivery. You can put those down — over there. And now you can go.

BEE: Do you know how intoxicatingly beautiful you are?

FRANNY: Now, *that's* a joke.

BEE: We find you unbearably sexy.

FRANNY: Who's we?

BEE: We know you haven't even begun to tap into your erotic capacity.

FRANNY: What's that smell?

BEE: That's my nectar.

FRANNY: Mmm. Not bad.

BEE: Franny Dambrose, you are wonderfully demanding, fascinatingly moody, exquisitely impossible to please.

FRANNY: Well —

BEE: Complicated, codependent, and controlling. Perfect in all ways.

FRANNY: Well —

BEE: We want to give you everything you always wanted, but thought you couldn't have: love, fulfillment, hot sex; we will serve your every need.

FRANNY: Well.

BEE: We want you to be our Queen.

FRANNY: What?

BEE: We've watched you. We've chosen you. We know you.

FRANNY: What is this?

BEE: You can run, but you can't hive. We even have a sense of humor.

FRANNY: Hardly.

BEE: Just think: You wouldn't have to work. You'd have plenty of time: to read, to lounge, to do your art. Think what you could paint with pollen.

FRANNY: That's very nice of you, but, hey why don't you get um, a real bee? I know you could find one, in um the park.

BEE: We had a bad experience. She was a . . . killer. So, we've opted for this scientifically advanced entomologically evolutionary revolutionary solution. We find a very special human female and offer her a better life. Works well for all involved.

FRANNY: If it works so well, what happened to your last one?

BEE: She fell in love with a Wasp. Not recommended. The children will be confused.

FRANNY: OK —.

BEE: Franny, imagine yourself. As Queen. You'd never be alone again on a Friday night. You'd be serving the greater good by helping to cross-pollinate. Not to mention, we will please you in every way. Have you ever thought about being with more than one male and their only pleasure is your pleasure?

FRANNY: Well. Um. Look, it's nothing personal, but I find you, I'm sorry to say, physically, uh, repulsive.

BEE: Oh, I think that could change.

FRANNY: And, I'm human.

BEE: That, too, can change. Amelia Earhart? She didn't disappear. She made a choice. So can you.

FRANNY: But what's wrong with being human?

BEE: Have you read the paper lately? Your species isn't exactly living up to its potential.

FRANNY: Amelia Earhart?

BEE: I don't want to rush you Franny, except that my brothers and cousins are eagerly waiting and time is quickly running out. Don't you want what I've offered? What is it you're reluctant to give up?

FRANNY: Well. My apartment.

BEE: A studio in Inwood?

FRANNY: It's near the subway.

BEE: You'd have your own hive.

FRANNY: My job.

BEE: That job sucks.

FRANNY: There are perks.

BEE: Like what?

FRANNY: Uh . . . Frequent-flyer miles.

BEE: You won't need those.

FRANNY: And there's Frank.

BEE: Frank is a fly, a gnat, a roach. Besides he's an actor. Forget Frank.

FRANNY: Believe me I've tried.

BEE: Franny oh Franny, have you looked at your life lately?

FRANNY: I prefer not to.

BEE: All of your qualities that absolutely don't work as a female human will work like gangbusters as a bee.

FRANNY: Things'll get better.

BEE: How long have you been saying that?

FRANNY: Time heals all wounds.

BEE: Then why are you still hurting? And why are you inflicting excruciating pain to your lovely legs? We like fuzzy!

FRANNY: Really?

BEE: Really. Weren't you the Queen in your grade school play? Didn't you enjoy it?

FRANNY: I loved it. But I didn't get to keep the crown. I wanted that crown.

BEE: You could have a crown.

FRANNY: But. Still. I'm terrified of you. I see a bee, I flee. It's a kind of a flight or flight kind of thing. I don't go on picnics, I avoid practically the entire outdoors because of you.

BEE: What exactly are you afraid of?

FRANNY: Pain, death, dying alone, that sort of thing.

BEE: Touch my stinger.

FRANNY: What?

BEE: Touch it.

FRANNY: No.

BEE: Don't you think it's time to change?

FRANNY: That's a pretty big change.

BEE: I know you, Franny Dambrose. The reason you're afraid of me is because
you *are* me. In your heart, you're a bee. Touch it.
(She touches it. Pulls her hand away. Twice. Touches it.)

FRANNY: Oh. Oh. It's — it's nice.

BEE: Isn't it?

FRANNY: It's mmm warm.

BEE: Yes.

FRANNY: Powerful.

BEE: Yes.

FRANNY: It's . . . growing.

BEE: Yes.

FRANNY: And that smell. Your . . . nectar.

BEE: Yes.
(A musical humming is heard. Lights change.)

FRANNY: That sound. What is it?

BEE: My cousins and brothers. Here to serve you.

FRANNY: Oh my. *(She feels them all over her body.)* What are they doing?

BEE: Touching you, tickling you, trying to please you.

FRANNY: Oh. Oh. *(The bee puts yellow stripes on her.)* What're those?

BEE: Your stripes.

FRANNY: They're so . . . soft. *(He puts antennae on her.)* Oh. *(He puts wings on
her.)* Oh. They're beautiful. I. Oh.
(The bee kisses her.)

FRANNY: I can't believe I kissed a bee. I feel . . . different. What's your name?

BEE: Dave the Bee.

FRANNY: Hi, Dave.
(The phone rings.)

BEE: Let it ring.

FRANNY: But. *(Ring.)*

BEE: Forget it.

FRANNY: But. *(Ring.)* It might be my boss. Or.

BEE: It's time.

FRANNY: But.

BEE: Let's go.

FRANNY: What if it's Frank?! *(She answers the phone.)* Hello? Frank?
(The lights change. The humming stops.)

FRANNY: *(Continued.)* I'm glad you called. What? You want me to stop calling? You're really happy since we broke up? You're still seeing my friend, Eleanor? You've asked her to marry you!? Great. That's just great. *(As Franny is about to burst into tears and launch an attack, Dave puts a crown on her head. Voila. She is transformed. She nearly drops the phone.)*

FRANNY: *(Continued.)* Frank, remember the Don't-bee and the Do-bee? Well, you are most definitely a Don't. And when it comes to you and your kind, I am done. *(She hangs up. She dials again.)* Buzz off!! *(She hangs up.)* *(Humming sounds. Lights change. Music. She kisses Dave.)*

FRANNY: OK, boys, let's fly.

END OF PLAY

2B (or Not 2B)

PART TWO

JACQUELYN REINGOLD

For Rich

2B (or Not 2B) Part 2 was first performed in the HB Short Play Festival 2004 at the HB Playwrights Theatre (William Carden, Artistic Director; Pamela Berlin, Playwrights Unit Director.) in New York City. It was directed by Michael Barakiva. Sets by David Korin; lights by Chris Dallos; costumes by Magge Lee-Burdoff; sound by Shane Rettig; Production Manager, Matt Britt; Production Stage Manager, Tiffany Tillman. The cast was: Franny: Jeanine Serralles; Manny: P. J. Sosko

CHARACTERS
   FRANNY: thirties. A Queen Bee. Used to be a human: female.
   MANNY: a really cute musician

PLACE
   A tasteful wedding

TIME
   Now

•   •   •

A wedding. Cocktail hour before the reception. Lights up on Franny, a human-sized Bee, wearing a tiara and holding a drink.

FRANNY: *(To the audience.)* I wasn't always a bee, I used to be a female human of a certain age with a certain career, but after Frank left me for Eleanor, a human female still fertile, I ran away with Dave, a large drone who recruited me to be the Queen by promising free room and board, all the hot sex I wanted with as many drones as I liked, and the diamond tiara I now wear on my head. That human, Frank, broke my heart in a million pieces and ruined my life in a million ways. Not that I blame him. Cause I don't. I know you're not supposed to. It's pathetic, it's unfeminist, it's the Goddamn truth. When he told me the most despicable things about his sorry life and threatened suicide, I gave him a lovely package of bath products, wrote out the number for the suicide hotline, and told him I would never leave. So he left me. For Eleanor, my former friend with a Ph.D. in semiotic videography who once dated one of the Baldwin brothers I forget which one, but he wasn't cute. When I told Frank that Eleanor had the papilloma virus in her mouth and her *vagina*, he thought I was lying, which I was, and stopped returning my calls. So when Dave, a strappingly handsome drone, came to my door and lured me with his luring talk, I converted. Entymologically. And being a bee is a helluva lot better than being a human female of a certain age and a certain career. Did you know that the young female worker bees are all sexually undeveloped? That the Queen is the only one who gets any? I've got the whole hive after my tail. I am their fucking Queen. Constantly. So when I heard through the grapevine — literally — that Frank and Eleanor were getting married, I thought I'd come by, make peace, and leave a jar of honey . . . laced with arsenic. Just kidding. I wouldn't do that. I've softened. I've rounded. I've changed — species. I help cross-pollinate now allowing fruit trees to flower, almonds to bud, and bleeding hearts to blossom. So I put on my dress wings, polished my crown, and caught the nearest tailwind to get here. I'll applaud the happy couple, say congratulations, then stick my stinger right up his married ass. Cause he's allergic, and he'll die! I've moved on from anger. Right into rage and revenge. Look at this. Even the flowers are tasteful, and I know flowers. And the music, perfect. They must have spent a fortune. I helped Frank get his ridiculously high-paying job and now he's rich, married, and I'm. A fat bee. I haven't heard music since I left humanity. All I've done is fuck drones. And catch up on old New Yorkers. Suck pollen. Not that I'm bitter. I'm sweet. Because I'm so filled with honey if you poked me I'd splat. I'm gonna shoot my poison into Frank's happy heart and halt its harmonious beating for good. I'll fuck it all up. Then leave mankind forever. Leave men forever. What is that music?? *(She yells toward the piano player.)* Hey, Music Guy cut it out! I might have to kill him, too. Hey Piano Boy! *(She freezes, stunned. To audience.)* OHMYGOD! He is so cute!

(Pianoboy enters.)

PIANOBOY: What's going on?

FRANNY: What is your problem playing music like that? I'm working up a maniacal rage.

PIANOBOY: Nice outfit.

FRANNY: Don't nice outfit me.

PIANOBOY: Your stripes too tight or something?

FRANNY: Don't bug me.

PIANOBOY: Would you like another drink?

FRANNY: You're probably gonna go hit on the girlfriends of the bride who feel like shit their friend is getting married but have to pretend they're happy. Look at them trying to attract your attention in their ridiculously short skirts and pathetically high heels.

PIANOBOY: It's a beautiful thing.

FRANNY: You probably think foreplay is to get a woman to stop thinking about her next pair of shoes.

PIANOBOY: Now that you mention it.

FRANNY: Buzz off.

PIANOBOY: Hey, you talked to me.

FRANNY: Just cause you're impossibly cute doesn't mean I'm attracted to you. I'm not even a human anymore.

PIANOBOY: I noticed.

FRANNY: I'm a bee. And I get plenty. I have no problem getting any. As a bee. I'm busy. As a bee.

PIANOBOY: *(He sings:)*
When you're passin' by . . . flowers drop and sigh
And I know the reason why
You're much sweeter . . . goodness knows
Honeysuckle rose

FRANNY: I can't imagine doing it with a human again —

PIANOBOY: Bee sex. How does that work?

FRANNY: — All those — limbs.

PIANOBOY: You get turned on by roundness of the shape?

FRANNY: And that — slippery skin.

PIANOBOY: Or the delicacy of the wing?

FRANNY: Women must jump all over you.

PIANOBOY: The taste of the royal jelly.

FRANNY: Those eyes. Those full lips.

PIANOBOY: The bend in your antennae.

FRANNY: That hair.

PIANOBOY: Your nectar.

FRANNY: Those peasant feet.

PIANOBOY: That buzz.

FRANNY: Your voice.

PIANOBOY: The way you fly.

FRANNY: The bulge in your fly.
(They jump on each other. Under the gift table.)

FRANNY: Just watch out for my stinger.

PIANOBOY: Watch out for mine!
(Their legs and arms stick out from under the table. Much activity.)

FRANNY/PIANOBOY: Buzz! Buzz! Oh! Oh! Oh! Buzz!
(They emerge.)

FRANNY: Wow, that was—
(She grabs him. They go at it again.)

FRANNY/PIANOBOY: Oh! Oh! Buzz! Buzz! Buzz! Oh!
(They emerge.)

FRANNY: Ohmygod that was great that was warm soft hard close intimate exquisite —

PIANOBOY: Yeah. Bee sex is hot.

FRANNY: I never knew it could feel like that. How did you do that?

PIANOBOY: I am all over your fuzz.

FRANNY: Skin sweat lips fingers. I haven't had fingers for forever.

PIANOBOY: What does a queen bee do all day anyway?

FRANNY: Pretty much fuck all the time.

PIANOBOY: You got it going on.

FRANNY: How am I gonna go back to drones?

PIANOBOY: How am I gonna go back to twenty year olds?

FRANNY: I long for you. I ache. I want to eat pastrami sandwiches chocolate ice cream, and sleep on a mattress together. I want to know all about you.

PIANOBOY: I like beer.

FRANNY: I like your knee joints your fatless butt and the fact that you walk don't fly.

PIANOBOY: Let's go to bars and make out.

FRANNY: Buy me a present.

PIANOBOY: How 'bout a piece of chocolate cake?

FRANNY: You have the best face I've ever seen.

PIANOBOY: You have great . . . bee boobies.

FRANNY: Are you seeing other women?

PIANOBOY: Not since we met.

FRANNY: My favorite playwright is Caryl Churchill.

PIANOBOY: My favorite monkey is the bonobo.

FRANNY: I love bonobos! Matriarchal society.

PIANOBOY: Yeah. Like how they have fuck all the time instead of fighting. I'm like that.

FRANNY: You are!?

PIANOBOY: Can I get your number? Maybe you could come over and we could you know get under the kitchen table.

FRANNY: You want my number!? It's — oh no I don't have a number! *(Sobs hysterically.)* I can't believe I finally meet a guy I like and I'm a bee!

PIANOBOY: Wow. That's a problem.

FRANNY: I can't be a human again. I'm irreversible!

PIANOBOY: I can't be a bee. I don't really like bees.

FRANNY: And I don't really like men.

PIANOBOY: I need a drink. You want something?

FRANNY: So now you're gonna leave? You're just gonna walk out and leave? Hit the road, put on your coat, take your marbles, your nasal spray, your scotch, and boogie-woogie back to your books your mountain bike your butterfly-catching kit?

PIANOBOY: I don't have any of those things. Well, I have a bike but —

FRANNY: I know you! You don't call or you call too much or you only call late at night.

PIANOBOY: I don't even have your number.

FRANNY: You're sweet only then to be cruel. You promise me a rose garden then refuse to buy me flowers.

PIANOBOY: I was just gonna get a beer. You want some wine?

FRANNY: If you're so smart why can't you understand that leaving at 6 AM with barely a word will hurt my feelings? And when you do stay, why do you wake me up by shouting "hey get up!"

PIANOBOY: Who are you talking about?

FRANNY: You're gonna pack your port, and go back to your wife, your girlfriend, your dog, your big house, your little apartment, your cabin, your villa, your kids, your antiques, your coffee plunger, your three-car garage, and your multiple sunglasses. When you said you were separated I thought it meant legally not physically. When you said you wanted children, I thought it meant with me. When you said you'd never leave I thought it meant — you'd never leave! You came into my life, defrosted the tundra of my heart and now I'll never hear from you again? I wait up for your calls I want your e-mails I send you erotic letters you don't answer —

PIANOBOY: We just met —

FRANNY: And it feels like forever! I can't believe after everything I've been through I'm here again. Hoping that you'll love me or like me or at least want to have sex with me on a semi regular basis. I love you I don't know how to live without you. Oh no! I'm feeling like a human female of a certain age and a certain career! No! NO! NO!

PIANOBOY: Hey hey hey, it's me, Pianoboy. I'm the only one here. Right? I'm your monkeyman who made you feel all good under the table. That's all I'm doing, right? I'm not those other guys. It's me — Bonoboboy. Come on. *(He kisses her.)* Hey, baby, honey pie, I don't even know your name.

FRANNY: It's Francesca. But you can call me Franny.

PIANOBOY: I'm Emanuel, but you can call me Manny.

FRANNY: Manny?

MANNY: Franny?

FRANNY: Manny?

MANNY: Franny?

FRANNY: Would you really have called?

MANNY: Sure.

FRANNY: How often?

MANNY: Couple times a week.

FRANNY: For how long?

MANNY: A while.

FRANNY: And then?

MANNY: Once a week. Every other week. Once a month. Maybe.

FRANNY: I'm so glad I'm not a human.

MANNY: I'm so glad I'm not married. That poor guy.

FRANNY: Frank!

MANNY: Yeah, the groom.

FRANNY: I completely forgot. I came here to kill him.

MANNY: Glad I got paid upfront.

FRANNY: All I wanted was for him to suffer.

MANNY: He's married, that'll take care of itself.

FRANNY: But now. I couldn't care less. I mean I still hope he has a short painful horrible life filled with suffering, misery, and hardship, but other than that I don't care. I haven't thought about him since we met. You changed my life.

MANNY: And you opened me up to a whole new world of insect copulation.

FRANNY: Manny, we can't stay together. The Bee/Human thing only leads to heartache. It's best if I go.

MANNY: You mean? Back to the hive?

FRANNY: God no, those drones wear me out.

MANNY: Other pastures?

FRANNY: Flying solo. You?

MANNY: I'm grooving.

FRANNY: You're a beautiful man.

MANNY: And you're a rockin' Queen. How 'bout a —

FRANNY: — Good-bye kiss?

(They kiss. It's hot.)

MANNY: Gimme a squeeze. *(She squeezes him. Hard.)* Whoa! How 'bout we —

FRANNY: — Go to your place? Just for tonight.

MANNY: I'm good with that.

FRANNY: Me too. I'll buzz off in the morning.

MANNY: I'll make you fuzzy buzzy til then.

FRANNY: I'm feeling fuzzy buzzy right now. Can we go?

MANNY: I still have to play for — forget it. Let's get a cab.

FRANNY: No need. Just get on my back and we'll fly.

MANNY: I got the keyboard, the amp, the mic —

FRANNY: Hop on. I can carry you. All of you. Come on, Pianoboy.

(He gets on her back.)

FRANNY: *(Continued.)* Let's fly.

(Spotlight on them. Singing. Flying.)

END OF PLAY

Aurolac Blues

SAVIANA STANESCU

CHARACTERS

ELVIS: nine, a Gypsy boy, street kid

MADONA: eight, a blond girl, street kid

They should be played by young adults in order to suggest the kids' premature maturity.

SETTING

On the sidewalk in Bucharest

• • •

Two Gypsy street-kids, Elvis and Madona, nine and eight, sit on the sidewalk in Bucharest, sniffing Aurolac (silver paint) from a plastic bag they pass to each other. They should be played by adults in order to suggest their premature maturity.

ELVIS: Madona. Madona! . . . I'm transforming myself . . . I can feel it . . . I am . . .

MADONA: You look the same.

ELVIS: Gimme your hand!

MADONA: Why?

ELVIS: Put it here, on my heart . . . *(She does so.)* Can you hear it?

MADONA: What?

ELVIS: My heart.

MADONA: No.

ELVIS: C'mon. You must hear it!

MADONA: I cannot hear with my hand.

ELVIS: I can.

MADONA: Elvis-the-liar! Elvis-the-liar!

ELVIS: Shhhhh . . . I don't want other people here when I am transforming myself . . .

MADONA: You're not . . .

ELVIS: In seven minutes it will be midnight. I'll change. You'll see.

MADONA: OK. You'll be a vampire. So what.

ELVIS: I won't need any food, any bed. I'll be sleeping in the cemetery. Hang out all night. With you.

MADONA: We already do that. No need to become a vampire.

ELVIS: I'll be strong. No one will beat me up. I'll bite everyone who dares to touch you. Or me.

MADONA: I bite them already.

ELVIS: But you don't kill them . . .

MADONA: I don't wanna kill them . . . Big Nose and Knife-guy are fun . . . when they don't touch me . . . They haven't touched me in a while . . .

ELVIS: Makarena is fun too.

MADONA: See. You don't wanna kill them.

ELVIS: I don't get it . . . why we call her Makarena. She dances makarena so badly . . .

MADONA: Exactly . . .

ELVIS: We call you Madona because you are beautiful. You look like her. I saw her on TV, at the shelter.

MADONA: I never saw her . . .

ELVIS: You should go to the shelter and ask them to let you see her.

MADONA: Now?

ELVIS: Tomorrow. At lunchtime. They will give us soup.

MADONA: Will you still eat soup? As a vampire, I mean.

ELVIS: Vampires eat soup too. They are like people, but they don't die and they have two longer teeth. These ones. (*He shows her.*)

MADONA: Only blood. They drink only blood. Makarena told me that.

ELVIS: You believe her or me?

MADONA: She's fifteen.

ELVIS: I don't really like blood . . .

MADONA: You will. (*Presses her hand on his chest.*) I think I can hear it now.

ELVIS: My heart?

MADONA: Yes . . . you're right, you're transforming yourself . . .

ELVIS: How do you know that?

MADONA: Your heart talks to me now.

ELVIS: It never talks to me. It only makes noises . . .

MADONA: She says that you must sing to me . . .

ELVIS: Sing what?

MADONA: An Elvis song, of course.

ELVIS: I can't sing.

MADONA: It doesn't matter. Sing to me!

ELVIS: I don't know his songs . . .

MADONA: Then walk like him, or talk like him . . . Why don't you try to transform yourself into him? A music star is funnier than a vampire . . .

ELVIS: I don't know him.

MADONA: C'mon . . . You never saw him on TV at the shelter?

ELVIS: I asked Mamma Annie to let me know when he's on, but she never did . . .

MADONA: You never spent more than an hour at the shelter . . .

ELVIS: Still . . .

MADONA: I slept there twice. They gave me a nice dress. Blue. With little flowers on it. I liked it a lot. It was like I was a garden or something. Everybody wanted to come closer to smell me, to touch me . . .

ELVIS: You didn't let them, did you?

MADONA: I sold the dress. To Makarena. She wears it as a blouse . . . She gave me two Aurolac bottles for it. Two!

ELVIS: Makarena is silly.

MADONA: C'mon, play Elvis, be Elvis!

ELVIS: I told you I don't know him!

MADONA: Your mom did. Do you think he's your father or something?

ELVIS: He's American, silly.

MADONA: So what. Mama Annie is American too.

ELVIS: When I'll be a vampire . . . I'll fly to America.

MADONA: You said you'd hang out here, with me. Liar!

ELVIS: I mean just for a night or so. To see the skyscrapers. The birds. The ocean. The city. I'm gonna eat a huge cheeseburger at McDonald's. With French fries. And Ketchup. And mayonnaise. And pickles. Like those at the McDonald's in Victoriei Square, but much bigger . . .

MADONA: I was there! I found a half-eaten hamburger on a table. Yummy.

ELVIS: *(Lost in his speech.)* Then I'm gonna play basketball with the black kids. I'll let them win. Then I will drive a limo. A long white limo. I'll be very elegant. I'll go to a roof-party and dance with women with diamonds around their necks. You know, movie stars. Glimmering and all that. Like real stars. Then I'm gonna look up at the sky and WOOF! Bite them . . . I saw that in a film at Victoria Cinema . . .

MADONA: They let you in?

ELVIS: I sneaked in there at night . . . slept in the restroom.

MADONA: How come they didn't catch you?

ELVIS: They did. "Stop that damn little gypsy, that little fucking thief!"

MADONA: What did you steal?

ELVIS: Nothing. But I bit them! I bit them and I ran away . . .

MADONA: You're something . . . Gimme the bag! *(She sniffs.)*

ELVIS: Don't take too much. I want you to see my transformation.

MADONA: Yeah . . .

ELVIS: It's starting. Touch my heart! Now!

MADONA: Yeah . . .

ELVIS: Ugh . . . Touch my back . . . Something happens to my back . . .

MADONA: *(Touching his back.)* Yeah?

ELVIS: Do you hear anything?

MADONA: Your back doesn't talk to me . . .

ELVIS: Ugh! . . . There, on the shoulder!

MADONA: I can feel something! It's like a . . . . I dunno . . .

ELVIS: It hurts . . .

MADONA: Do you want me to sing for you or something?

ELVIS: You can't sing . . .

MADONA: Sometimes I can . . . *(She starts singing a nice lullaby.)*

ELVIS: My head hurts too . . .

MADONA: Take some . . . . you'll feel better. *(She passes the Aurolac bag.)*

ELVIS: Can you feel anything there, on my back? Something is biting me . . .
like from inside . . . Like two dogs trying to get out of me . . .
(Elvis is sniffing more Aurolac.)

MADONA: Shhhh . . . You're turning into a vampire. You'll travel to America. You'll
bring me a photo of Madonna. With autograph. Tell her to write "For
Madona, with love." No. Tell her to write just "For Madona." No. Tell her
to write only her name. And ask her for a dress. I think she'd send me a dress.
She has too many. She will send me a dress, won't her? I think she will. I'm
sorry I don't have a photo of myself to send her. But I must learn to write
my name first. Tomorrow I'm going to the shelter to learn to write my name.
I promise. Remind me to keep my promise . . . Hey, Elvis! Fuck!

ELVIS: What?

MADONA: Leave some for me! You won't need it anymore.
(She grabs the bag and sniffs.)

ELVIS: Transforming . . . I am . . . into . . . transform . . .

MADONA: What are those Elvis? Those things on your back . . .

ELVIS: Oh, it doesn't hurt me anymore. It passed.

MADONA: Elvis . . . there are two . . . on your back!

ELVIS: I feel better. I dunno. I feel light.

MADONA: Elvis . . . they are growing! Don't look back, they are growing!

ELVIS: I feel like singing . . .

MADONA: They are silver . . . Vampire's wings are supposed to be black or red,
aren't they?

ELVIS: I'm going home now.

MADONA: We don't have a home.

ELVIS: To America.

MADONA: Elvis . . . your face is silver . . . you've turned into a . . . an . . . a . . . an . . .

ELVIS: Nonsense.

(Elvis begins to mumble a soft song (to be chosen by the actor).

MADONA: Something went wrong. You've turned into an angel, Elvis! An angel!

END OF PLAY

A Medical Breakthrough

FREDERICK STROPPEL

A Medical Breakthrough was produced by The Theatre Artists Workshop of Westport in Norwalk, Conn., in October 2005, as part of their annual Playwrights One-Act Festival. It was directed by E. Katherine Kerr, and it had the following cast: Dr. Fields: Joanne Parady; Mr. Moore: Chilton Ryan

CHARACTERS
DR. FIELDS
MR. MOORE

SETTING
A medical office

• • •

Dr. Fields sits at her office desk, making an entry on a medical chart. When she finishes, she sits back.

DR. FIELDS: Next!
(Mr. Moore enters, walking carefully.)
DR. FIELDS: Ah, Mr. Moore? I'm Dr. Fields.
(Shakes his hand.)
What seems to be the problem?
MR. MOORE: *(Unsettled.)* You're Dr. Fields?
DR. FIELDS: That's right.
MR. MOORE: Oh — I didn't realize . . .
DR. FIELDS: You didn't realize I would be a woman. A common reaction, unfortunately. No one expects a woman to gravitate to the field of proctology. It is considered a male domain. And yet we think it quite natural for a woman to be a gynecologist. As they say in baseball, it's a game of inches. Please, take a chair.
MR. MOORE: *(Hesitant.)* Well, I . . .
DR. FIELDS: Don't worry. It's a special pneumatic seat. It cushions the meanest hemorrhoid in a cloud of velvet. Like sitting on cotton candy, I'm told.
MR. MOORE: I don't have hemorrhoids.
DR. FIELDS: Everyone has hemorrhoids, Mr. Moore. Some are active, and some are sleeping, waiting . . . Like volcanoes.
MR. MOORE: Perhaps so, but that's not the cause of my immediate distress. You see . . . Well, this is rather embarrassing . . .
DR. FIELDS: No need for modesty here. We're talking about a simple body orifice, as normal and necessary as an ear or a nostril, as elemental as earth, wind, and fire. We're both adults, are we not? No reason why we can't confront this issue head-on, maturely and objectively.
MR. MOORE: I guess you're right. Well, here goes. I, uh . . . I have a foreign object lodged in my rectal cavity.
DR. FIELDS: You have something stuck up your ass?

(Mr. Moore is startled.)

Excuse me if I strike an air of slangy informality. I find it helps ease the tension. Now, I don't want to know how this object got where it got — your personal life is your own, and you are welcome to it. Just tell me this: Is it alive?

MR. MOORE: No.

DR. FIELDS: Good! That's half the battle right there.

(Takes notes.)

Now — was this an accidental or deliberate insertion?

MR. MOORE: Uh . . . Deliberate.

DR. FIELDS: Unilateral, or with the aid of an outside agent?

MR. MOORE: There were a number of us . . . But I don't want you to get the wrong idea. It was not a form of sexual byplay.

DR. FIELDS: *(A practiced smile.)* The thought never entered my mind.

MR. MOORE: See, I was at this party with the guys, and we were sitting around, drinking . . . Eddie — the host — his wife just had a baby, and we got into a discussion about childbirth and labor pains, and that somehow drifted into speculation about the comparative elasticity of various orifices — orifi? — . . . Anyway, hypothesis evolved into experimentation, one thing followed upon another . . . And here I am, the sorry man you see before you today.

DR. FIELDS: Was this a Super Bowl Party?

MR. MOORE: Yes.

DR. FIELDS: I can't tell you how many customers I get the day after the Super Bowl. Practically epidemic. What is it, one of those little rubber footballs?

MR. MOORE: No.

DR. FIELDS: A bottle of Heineken? A can of Pringles?

MR. MOORE: I don't think you're going to guess.

DR. FIELDS: Mr. Moore, I'm a seasoned proctologist. You can't imagine the things I've pulled out of there. It's not a pine cone, is it? Because that, believe me, is the worst-case scenario.

MR. MOORE: No, it's . . . well, it's a hand grenade.

DR. FIELDS: A hand grenade?

MR. MOORE: I'm afraid so.

DR. FIELDS: Well, now! That *is* impressive. A hand grenade! You're right, I never would have guessed.

MR. MOORE: Eddie being a former marine, he has a wide assortment of war souvenirs. This one hails from Grenada, ironically.

DR. FIELDS: *(Writing.)* Just let me get all this down . . .

(Chuckles.)

"Grenada" — very good. I have to tell you, Mr. Moore, this is quite original — perhaps unprecedented. It will make a most distinguished addition to the growing treasury of proctological lore. You should be very proud.

MR. MOORE: I'm a little ambivalent about the whole thing. You see — it's apparently a live grenade. Capable of detonation.

DR. FIELDS: *(Sits back.)* You have a live grenade in your rectum? Well, that ups the ante considerably, doesn't it?

MR. MOORE: That's why I insisted on seeing you before lunch. There's a sense of urgency here that I can't over-emphasize.

DR. FIELDS: To be sure. Now I'm intrigued — whatever possessed you to shove a loaded hand grenade up there? This couldn't have been a casual impulse.

MR. MOORE: I guess you could blame it on peer pressure. The other guys were showing off their respective capacities, and I felt the need to hold up my end. Plus, I admit, I do have a fierce competitive streak. If Andy Landis could manage a Chia pet, well . . . it's a cold day in hell when he can get the better of me.

DR. FIELDS: Are you in any pain?

MR. MOORE: I'm hardly comfortable. But my pressing concern is the pin. It's in a delicate position. So delicate as to preclude any attempt at exercise or basic hygiene. One false move — an errant turn, a sudden sneeze . . .

DR. FIELDS: You're saying your butt could blow at any time.

MR. MOORE: I'm on the verge of implosion, yes.

DR. FIELDS: You're sitting on a powder keg.

(She chuckles.) This little experiment could really backfire on you, hm?

MR. MOORE: *(Nettled.)* Dr. Fields, I must say, I find your breeziness somewhat inappropriate. I have an unstable hand grenade embedded in my rectum. I'm under considerable stress.

DR. FIELDS: Mr. Moore, laughter is the best medicine. Let me tell you a little story. We had a patient in here once with serious blockage issues. He was what we in the business call "morbidly constipated." It seems this fellow had a nervous habit of eating twine, and all that loose fiber had collected and solidified in the colonic well. He was literally bound up. Well, we tried everything — vaseline, scissors, a small chisel — nothing worked. The little mother wasn't going to budge. So we took a break, and just to relieve the tension, we started telling a few jokes. There was one about a priest and a duck — or was it a quail? — I forget, but anyway, we had this fellow laughing to beat the band, doubled over, pounding on the desk, . . . Finally he gave one good hearty snort, and let me tell you, that thing shot out of him like a bazooka. Put a dent in that wall over there. You can still see it.

MR. MOORE: Where did he get all the twine?

DR. FIELDS: I don't know — Home Depot? — that's not important. The point I'm making is, you have to maintain your sense of humor. So you have a hand grenade in your ass — it's not the end of the world.

MR. MOORE: I'm sorry. I'm just feeling a bit overmatched.

DR. FIELDS: Have you spoken with a military consultant? Perhaps it can be easily disarmed.

MR. MOORE: I stopped by the Army Recruiting Center. They wouldn't even look at it — considered my recreational use of military arsenal to be disrespectful and subversive. The local police informed me that I could be brought up on charges for carrying a concealed weapon. No, I'm really at my wit's end here, Dr. Fields. Only you can help me.

DR. FIELDS: *(Rises.)* And I will do my very best. Of course, these are unusual circumstances, and I can't promise anything . . .

(Cheerful.) On the other hand, I've never lost a patient yet. Let's go to the examination table and take a look, shall we?

(Mr. Moore and Dr. Fields go behind a small screen.)

DR. FIELDS: *(Behind the screen.)* Just loosen your pants and bend over.

(Beat.)

OK. Now open wide, and say "ah." Just kidding.

(Beat.)

Ah, yes. I see our little guest. Hello there! Want to come out and play? *(Reassuringly.)* Well, Mr. Moore, if it's any comfort to you, it doesn't look nearly as bad as it probably feels. I'm relatively confident that we can discharge the grenade without surgery. But it's going to take a major commitment from you.

MR. MOORE: I'm willing to do whatever it takes.

DR. FIELDS: All right. I want you to squeeze my hand very hard. Now, take short quick breaths. Like this.

(She demonstrates. We hear Mr. Moore following her example.)

DR. FIELDS: Now Push!

(Mr. Moore grunts.)

DR. FIELDS: Now short breaths . . .

(More short breaths.) Now PUSH!

(He grunts with greater force.) Short breaths . . .

(Short breaths.) PUSH!

(Mr. Moore gives a horrendous moan. Beat.)

DR. FIELDS: I think it moved. Just rest a minute. Let me get the forceps.

MR. MOORE: Please be careful.

DR. FIELDS: Don't worry. If I can just hook on to this . . .

(A small metallic clink, as something hits the floor.)

MR. MOORE: *(Concerned.)* What was that?

(Beat.)

DR. FIELDS: Holy Jesus! The pin . . . ! He's gonna BLOW!

(Dr. Fields suddenly rushes from behind the screen and out the front door. A long beat, before she peeks in again.)

MR. MOORE: I think it was just your earring.

(Dr. Fields feels her ear, realizes he is right. She sheepishly returns.)

DR. FIELDS: Of course, how silly. That clip is always coming loose.

(Looking around.) Now, where did I put those forceps?:

MR. MOORE: I believe they're still in there.

DR. FIELDS: Oh! Right you are. OK, let's go for one more big push. Ready? — PUSH!

MR. MOORE: NNNNNGGGGGHHHH!!!

DR. FIELDS: Here it comes! I see it! Yes! YESSSSS . . . !

MR. MOORE: *(A primal groan.)* OOOOOOOHHHHHHHH . . . ..!

(Dr. Fields emerges from behind the screen, flushed and breathless. She holds the hand grenade in a towel. Exhausted, she sits back down at her desk.)

DR. FIELDS: Whew! Oh, baby. What a ride.

(Mr. Moore enters now, adjusting his belt. He is drained but relieved.)

DR. FIELDS: How are you feeling, Mr. Moore?

MR. MOORE: Depleted. For a moment there my whole life flashed before me.

DR. FIELDS: Thank God it didn't flash behind you.

(They laugh heartily.) Ah, well. We can laugh now. You might want to use a stool-softener for the next few days, and avoid any Mexican food.

MR. MOORE: I want you to know that I appreciate all that you've done for me. You really went the extra yard.

DR. FIELDS: I'm just glad it all ended happily.

MR. MOORE: Does it have to end?

DR. FIELDS: Pardon?

MR. MOORE: *(Takes her hand.)* Dr. Fields — you must know that something special has passed between us.

DR. FIELDS: Mr. Moore, please —

MR. MOORE: You can't pretend it didn't happen. Back there I felt something deeper with you than with any other woman I've known.

DR. FIELDS: A simple adrenaline rush brought on by intense physical stress . . .

MR. MOORE: No, it was more than that! It was magic, it was moonbeams . . . And we can't let it die! We can't! It has to go on!

DR. FIELDS: No, no . . . !

(Sighs.) Oh, why does it always have to end this way?

MR. MOORE: *(Crestfallen.)* Always? You mean — I'm not the first?

DR. FIELDS: Mr. Moore, you have to understand — today was something new for you. And it was strange and thrilling, and maybe it expanded your horizons a little. But that's my world, every day. That's my center, my touchstone, the polestar around which my universe wheels. You're going back to your everyday life with a new experience under your belt, but I'm here for the long run. A proctologist, c'est moi. I'm not sure if you can deal with that.

MR. MOORE: *(Bitterly.)* Fancy words. But what you're saying is, you don't want me. What is it, that I'm too small? Too raw?

DR. FIELDS: *(An appreciative smile.)* You're magnificent. You remind me of why I entered this challenging field in the first place. But we're not meant to be, that's all. It's apples and oranges.

MR. MOORE: When I walked in here today, I was desperate. But you gave me hope, gave me a reason to carry on. And now you yank it away. God, I feel so empty. If I could run out of here, I would.

(A painful silence. Dr. Fields holds up the grenade.)

DR. FIELDS: May I keep this? As a souvenir?

MR. MOORE: *(Shrugs.)* I don't think Eddie would want it back now, anyway.

DR. FIELDS: Thank you. I'll treasure it.

(A look passes between them.) Go now, and don't look back.

(Mr. Moore exits carefully. Dr. Fields looks tenderly at the grenade, gently puts it on the desk. She composes herself, takes up her clipboard.)

DR. FIELDS: Next . . . !

(As she waits bravely, the lights dim.)

END OF PLAY

Brother/Bar

JEFF TABNICK

CHARACTERS
  NICK: Male, twenty-three
  ERIN: female, twenty-two

TIME
  Present

PLACE
  A bar

• • •

Nick and Erin sit together at the bar. He drinks water. She drinks beer.

NICK: *(Too insistent.)* If *I* lived there, I'd have penguins.
  (Nick laughs too loudly at his own joke.)
ERIN: In upstate New York?
NICK: I LOVE penguins.
  (Nick laughs again.)
ERIN: They're cute enough.
NICK: The best of all the animals.
ERIN: Well I like polar —
NICK: *(Interrupting her, insistent.)* Like that cartoon in *The New Yorker.* My
  mom gets it.
ERIN: *(Remembering, no attitude attached.)* You live at home.
NICK: Un-huh.
ERIN: I didn't mean it like that.
NICK: It would be stupid to be anywhere else right now.
ERIN: *(As if she is warming up to tell a story.)* I don't think I could, me, see —
NICK: One penguin is *flying,* and he's looking down at all the other penguins
  that are *standing* and he shouts down to them, "We just weren't flapping
  hard enough." Oh come on that's good.
ERIN: I *get* it.
NICK: It's good.
ERIN: Why is your brother staring at us from across the bar?
NICK: I'm talking to . . . someone.
ERIN: You don't talk to people?
NICK: My brother doesn't think I talk to people.
ERIN: He looks worried.

NICK: I'm too loud indoors and I talk about pinching a loaf — that's what he thinks, he thinks I'd do that around people.

ERIN: And you wouldn't?

NICK: He thinks I've never had a . . . girlfriend. He thinks I'll meet a small Asian woman.

ERIN: There's nothing wrong with Asian women.

NICK: When I'm in my *thirties*. She will be the first woman to get me off so I will marry her. And then we will have biracial super babies.

ERIN: He told you he thinks that?

NICK: *My dad* thinks I'm schizophrenic or depressed or — retarded, and that I should be evaluated and put on drugs and — . He told my brother that, but my brother told my father he's trying to fix a delicate problem with a sledgehammer.

ERIN: *(Underneath, trailing off.)* And then did your brother tell you your father told him he thinks you're — ?

NICK: *(Continuous.)* So my brother decides to try to be a little more proactive so he invites me up to stay with him for a while and he takes me out with all of his boring friends to all of these boring bars even though I don't drink and he tries to introduce me to girls not really hot girls but girls I'd have a chance with —

ERIN: That's not very nice.

NICK: And so here we are at your brother's, my brother's friend's, birthday party in a bar.

(Awkward silence. Erin considers getting up but he begins to speak — .)

NICK: The last time I saw you was at your house, your family didn't live close to ours, my brother was visiting your brother, and we picked him up after he was there for a weekend, when I was thirteen and you were twelve and you and I sat in the same room for an hour and said nothing and did nothing.

ERIN: Maybe you're gay.

NICK: They wish, they're both practically gay themselves, my father and my brother, my father just learned the term *metrosexual* and uses it when referring to himself in the third person. I don't brush my teeth or shower regularly, I'm not gay.

ERIN: *(Trying to laugh it off.)* That's disgusting.

NICK: I didn't shower today.

ERIN: Come on.

NICK: I'm *clean* though. My brother can't figure it out. Was it our unhappy childhood? Did we even have an unhappy childhood, he read one theory that it's your relationship with your sibling that determines who you will be, but he's sure that's not true, he's not even sure there's anything wrong with me.

ERIN: Is there anything wrong with you?

NICK: I'm very closed off.

ERIN: I didn't realize.

NICK: A year ago I graduated college, I didn't go to medical school like I was supposed to, I moved back home, I never told anybody why. I show no emotion. I don't have any friends. I don't look for a job. My mother cries and screams and threatens to throw me out of the house and I don't seem to care, I don't say anything or if I do, I say I'm going to fill out grad school applications but neither of us *does* anything, me or my mother. I refuse to talk about myself.

ERIN: You're doing plenty of that tonight.

NICK: I'm not talking to you about these things. I'm telling you jokes I read in magazines or I'm telling you about pranks I pulled in college. Or I'm not talking to you at all.

ERIN: But you're saying all these things —

NICK: *(Nearly continuous.)* He thinks that maybe I don't feel empathy like other people do. But what should he do? Should he respect my privacy, recognize he's not my parent and leave me alone or should he badger me about getting a job, getting a girlfriend, getting out there in the world. You hear these stories in the news, these outrageous stories. A quiet young man stabs his own mother to death in her bed on a humid night in the heavily shaded suburbs. And in the morning when he's picked up on the highway with blood on his boots, all his old college professor can say to the news is ". . . if only someone had encouraged him to form relationships." But then you see another quiet young man on Court TV and you see his meddlesome brother constantly badgering him, "Why don't you have a girlfriend, why don't you go out at all," and all the quiet young man hears is what's wrong with you? And all he wants is to experience life in his own way. He's just a late bloomer, he needs to watch the clouds go by, after all if his parents allow him to live in the house without a job, why *should* he get a job until he's good and ready? But his brother's badgering finally convinces him that something *is* wrong with him and so then he goes and picks up a prostitute because obviously he *should* be with a woman, she laughs at his ineptitude so yes, indeed! something *is* wrong with him, and then he hits her, but only once, but not knowing his own strength he kills her! and ends up in jail for manslaughter! Fulfilling the role his brother has created for him! So, you see, don't you? If you leave me alone, I'll kill my mother, if you badger me, I'll kill a prostitute. All roads lead to violent death.

ERIN: So why are you talking to me about all of these *things* if you're so closed off?

NICK: *(Reasonably.)* This is a play . . .

ERIN: *(Underneath.)* So?

NICK: *(Continuous.)* . . . a play that my brother is writing *and* this is a real event. But all he can do is watch the real event from across the bar, he can't hear it and with all the people in between he can barely see it.

ERIN: *Who* am I?

NICK: He's not interested in you.

ERIN: He's not?

NICK: You're upset?

ERIN: Only in his play.

NICK: As we really talk?

ERIN: I think he's ingratiating.

NICK: Still his words.

ERIN: It's sad that your brother finds himself ingratiating.

NICK: He's trying to elicit sympathy. In a play about me nonetheless. I don't talk anything like this!

ERIN: He thinks you think he'd do that to elicit sympathy.

NICK: He thinks he thinks he'd do that to elicit sympathy. Let's just push on . . .

ERIN: They're his words, what's the point?

NICK: . . . to get to know each other better? I don't see any other choice. OK. So far it's been OK enough.

(Beat.)

ERIN: Well I need him to write me a little more specifically, he's been very vague about my point of view on you.

NICK: He thinks you've gotten sexier as you've gotten older but you look like a female version of your brother.

ERIN: What about my *personality?*

NICK: He's just thinking about what hot actress will play you and he's probably playing with himself.

ERIN: Oh I'm starting to know who I am.

NICK: What do you mean?

ERIN: He's giving me a point of view on you.

NICK: Are you someone who will continue to talk to me?

ERIN: He doesn't think that would be realistic.

NICK: *Now* he's after realism?

ERIN: It's not going to be good from here on in.

NICK: Why not?

ERIN: He's not writing me as someone who's nice to someone like you. But really believe me, I was hoping he would write me as . . . a small Asian woman.

NICK: I'm not in my thirties yet. Just tell me, whatever you are going to say that's mean, you won't really mean it.

ERIN: Of course I'm going to mean it, it's who I am! Tell me a college prank.

NICK: I don't want to.

ERIN: *You said it yourself* — you told me a joke from a magazine, now tell me a college prank.

NICK: Or I'm not talking to you at all. I said that too.

(Beat.)

NICK: *(Hesitantly.)* At this one party we had at a friend of ours' house in college, there was this kid there, I don't know I just didn't like him. He was just a dork, I mean we didn't know him. He was just annoying.

ERIN: Un-huh.

(Erin flashes him a big fake smile and looks around for a way to get away from him. Nick noticed but continues on.)

NICK: I was bartending at the party, I always bartended at the parties.

(Erin starts to get up.)

ERIN: Look —

NICK: *(Insistent.)* The joke is good! So I took all the dregs of other people's finished drinks and gave this dork a full glass of them all mixed together.

ERIN: Why?

NICK: *(Annoyed.)* He was annoying!

ERIN: *(Slightly laughing at him, patronizing.)* OK, calm down.

NICK: Then he got sick and threw up outside.

ERIN: *(Impatient.)* And you all laughed.

NICK: No one knew I did it but me. I laughed. Come on that's good.

ERIN: *(Visibly disturbed.)* I *get* it. OK?

NICK: It's good. I told people later, later I told people and they thought it was good. You tell me a story.

ERIN: Look, I've gotta —

NICK: You don't have any stories?

ERIN: I studied a lot in college.

NICK: How can you not have any stories? Not even one story?

(Erin smiles a big fake smiles and gets up.)

NICK: I studied a lot, I studied more than any of the people I lived with that are going to medical school now, I haven't heard you tell one story.

ERIN: I should go talk to my brother and then I'm going home, I'm tired. It was good to see you again.

(Nick nods not looking at her.)

(Erin gets up and exits.)

(She sneaks back onstage.)

ERIN: Well that wasn't so bad.

NICK: What do you mean?

ERIN: He knows I'm here?

NICK: Of course.

ERIN: I was worried for a second that I was going to be really destructive, say something I was really thinking. Your brother was very kind to you in that scene. I was just dismissive really. And you were resigned.

NICK: Realism?

ERIN: I should go talk to my brother and then I'm going home, I'm tired. It was good to see you again.

(Erin starts to exit.)

NICK: So this is what happened?

ERIN: He's just writing it.

NICK: But he knows . . .

ERIN: Unless he doesn't know.

NICK: I guess that's the hope.

(Blackout.)

END OF PLAY

Foul Territory

CRAIG WRIGHT

CHARACTERS
    OWEN: thirties to forties
    RUTH: thirties to forties

SETTING
    A row of far left-field seats at Yankee Stadium

. . .

The scene is a row of far left-field seats at Yankee Stadium. Owen (thirties to forties) is seated next to Ruth (thirties to forties). Throughout the scene we can hear a baseball game in progress; the distant drone of the announcer giving the play-by-play; the general crowd roar; and the periodic crack of the bat hitting the ball. Owen and Ruth are both eating popcorn or peanuts.
We hear the crack of the bat hitting the ball. Ruth jumps out of her seat.

RUTH: Yeah, Bernie! Way to go! Way to bloop that ball in there!!!
    (She settles back into her seat.)
    I think they're gonna do it this year, Owen. I can feel it. They're going all the way. Three months from now, mark my words, it's the World Series, and we'll be sitting here winnin' it . . .
    (She eats a mouthful of popcorn, then finishes her thought with her mouth full.)
ANNOUNCER: NOW BATTING . . . NUMBER TWO . . . DEREK JETER.
RUTH: Mark my words.
    (Another big mouthful — and She turns to Owen — .)
RUTH: Don'tcha think?
    (— to catch him eyeing her with pity.)
RUTH: What? What are you looking at? What?
OWEN: *(After a beat, pityingly.)* You're so brave.
RUTH: Gimme a break.
OWEN: No, I mean it, Ruth, you are —
RUTH: Because I think the *Yankees* have a chance? It doesn't take a genius —
OWEN: No, to be out here like this, like you are.
RUTH: At the game?
OWEN: At the game, at the whole thing!
    (We hear the crack of the bat hitting the ball.)
OWEN: To be getting back on your feet the way you're getting — after what Tom did to you — you're so sweet and brave —

(He eats a single piece of popcorn, gazing at her. She tracks the approaching ball with her eyes.)

OWEN: — so sweet and brave.

RUTH: Stop it.

OWEN: No, I mean it, you're, like, straight outta Laura Ingalls Wilder, I'm so proud of you, to bounce back like this. After Monty left me —
(A ball sails in and cracks Owen loudly on the head — .)

OWEN: OW!

RUTH: Oh God! Oh God, Owen, are you alright? Oh God!

OWEN: *(Holding his head.)* I'm fine, I'm fine —

RUTH: Didn't you see that coming?

OWEN: Yeah, I, I kinda did . . .

RUTH: It was coming right at you —

OWEN: I know —

RUTH: Oh my God . . . do you need anything? Ice, or —

OWEN: No —

RUTH: Should we take you to First Aid or something?

OWEN: No, I'm fine! I'm good. Really. Just watch your game, honey. Enjoy yourself. It's your night. It's your night.

RUTH: You're sure?

OWEN: Yes —

RUTH: Because we can go, really —

OWEN: *(Still rocking, in terrible pain.)* No, I'm shakin' it off. I'm a trooper. I'm fine.

RUTH: *(Double-checking.)* You're absolutely sure?

OWEN: Yes.

RUTH: *(Doubtfully.)* OK. OK. You're sure you're alright?

OWEN: Yep. Par for the course. I'm fine.

RUTH: OK. OK.

(She settles back into watching the game. A moment passes. Something catches her eye.)

RUTH: Did you see that?

OWEN: No, what?

RUTH: He balked. *(To the field.)* Stay on the rubber! *(After a long beat.)* Look, he did it again —
(She stands and screams at the field.)

RUTH: *Stay on the rubber! This isn't Cuba, pal! (To Owen.)* Do you see what I'm talkin' about?

OWEN: *(Still rubbing his head.)* No, I — I missed it —

RUTH: He balks, like, every third pitch, this guy, and no one calls it! No one ever calls it! *(Amazed.)* Jesus.

(She sits back down, eats some popcorn.)

RUTH: What's the point of having a rule if no one's gonna call it?

OWEN: Have you heard from him? At all?

RUTH: I don't want to talk about it —

OWEN: Wouldja take him back?

RUTH: No!

(We hear the crack of the bat hitting the ball.)

RUTH: You don't get it, Owen, Tom Scintilla leaving me is the *best thing* that ever could have happened — to me or the kids —

OWEN: But you miss him —

RUTH: I don't —

OWEN: Oh, come on, you miss him and you want him back, just admit it. When Monty left me —

(The ball sails in and hits him hard in the face.)

OWEN: OW!!

RUTH: *(Angry and concerned.)* Owen, move!!

(Blood sprays from his nose. He clutches it in agony.)

OWEN: When?

RUTH: *When you see the ball coming!* God! Are you alright? You're bleeding!

OWEN: I am?

RUTH: Is anything broken?

OWEN: No, it just . . . it just kinda . . . *hurts* . . .

(She pulls a napkin from her popcorn container and anxiously dabs his nose, trying to soak up some of the blood.)

OWEN: Ow, ow, ow . . .

RUTH: *(After a beat, with one eye on the game.)* So you saw that coming?

OWEN: Of course!

RUTH: So why didn't you *move?*

OWEN: What would be the point?

RUTH: What the hell does that mean? Jesus —

(She suddenly stands up and screams at the field.)

RUTH: *Would someone please nail this guy's feet to the motherfuckin' rubber or make the call??* Jesus Christ!

(Ruth sits back down, annoyed with the game.)

RUTH: I mean, this guy's not gonna cost us the game, but *shit!*

(A moment passes as She eats some popcorn and looks at Owen.)

RUTH: So what do you mean, "what would be the point?"

OWEN: It doesn't matter —

RUTH: Sure it does —

OWEN: No, you're enjoying the game —

RUTH: No, tell me! I've been going to baseball games for thirty-five years, Owen, I never caught a foul ball once and I just saw you get hit twice in one game!

OWEN: That's life —

RUTH: No, it's not life, it's fuckin' weird! *(Then, responding approvingly to the field.)* Ball four! There! Thank you! Thank you! *(To Owen.)* Do you realize, now, with Bernie and Derek on base, if A-Rod hits a home run, it's over, right?

OWEN: Yeah —

RUTH: This is a good game — All right! They're changing pitchers! Take a hike, you bum!

OWEN: When I got hit in the face with a baseball the *first* time —

RUTH: *(Caught offguard.)* How many times have you been hit?

OWEN: I don't know, a lot.

RUTH: You never told me this —

OWEN: It never came up — we never went to a game —

RUTH: I guess you're right —

OWEN: — the first time I was eleven years old, trying to catch a pop fly in the street —

RUTH: You played baseball?

OWEN: I know, it's unlikely —

RUTH: It's mega-unlikely —

OWEN: Well, I did, and this kid hit a pop fly and I must have misjudged or something, the important part is BANG, I got hit right between the eyes.

RUTH: Ouch.

OWEN: Yeah. There was blood everywhere, my eyes were swollen shut —

RUTH: God —

OWEN: Yeah, and I got totally got spooked.

(He blows his nose and the napkin fills with blood.)

RUTH: Are you sure you're alright?

OWEN: Yeah, I just feel a little . . . a little faint, anyway, a couple days later, I was at a baseball game for my school — not even playing, I was just doing stats, because my vision was still a little screwed up, and Jonny Blank hit a high foul and I freaked out. Everyone else was just sitting there, and I'm screaming, running around like a bee is chasing me and I'm ALREADY crying and I finally find the spot where I'm safe and I crouch down and cover my ears, but then I hear somebody catch it, so I look up and BANG, it hits me in the face!

RUTH: Oh my God!

OWEN: I know!

RUTH: What are the chances?

OWEN: Very high, obviously —

RUTH: *(Affirmatively.)* I guess —

OWEN: Anyway, I spent the next week in the hospital.

RUTH: The hospital?

OWEN: Kind of a . . . mental hospital —

RUTH: Oh —

OWEN: — and when I got out, my father, my beloved father whom I must have generated in my previous life in some evil DUNGEON, fabricated him from trash like some Golem, you know, to torture me later in case I forgot what was true about GOD, my beloved father decided to take me to a baseball game. He told me I had to get back on the horse. I cried the whole way in the car, "Don't take me. Turn around. I want to go home." He didn't care. We got to the game and lo and behold —

RUTH: You got hit —

OWEN: No. Nothing happened. *(After a beat.)* For eight innings.

RUTH: Oh no —

OWEN: And then Lou Piniella hit a high foul into the stands, and my father said "Just sit still," and I did — for two seconds — and then I RAN up the stairs into an empty row that looked safe and BANG, it caught me right in the ear!

RUTH: No!

OWEN: Yes! I still can't hear anything in this ear! I point this ear at something, I hear the ocean. MAYBE.

RUTH: That's amazing.

ANNOUNCER: NOW BATTING . . . NUMBER THIRTEEN . . . ALEX RODRIGUEZ.

OWEN: We can't run, Ruth, that's my point. Whether it's baseballs or heart-break, whether it's your Tom or my Monty, there's no escaping it. Life is going to destroy us. It's going to. Letting it happen is the only freedom we have.

RUTH: But Owen, that's absurd —

OWEN: It's the truth!

RUTH: But Owen, I'm happier now than I've been in ten years! The house is clean, all of Tom's stupid model train stuff is outta there; the kids are doing better in school; Carla Kendall is setting me up next week with a really nice guy —

OWEN: *(Doubtful.)* Oh, right —

RUTH: He sounds really sweet, he's a personal trainer —

OWEN: Sure he is —

RUTH: I think things are really looking up!

OWEN: And I think you're kidding yourself! I think you're seriously kidding yourself.

(We hear a loud crack of the bat hitting the ball.)

OWEN: *(Fatalistically.)* See, here it comes again —

(Ruth stands up.)

RUTH: Catch it!

OWEN: No, there's no point!

RUTH: Owen, stand up, put out your hands and catch it!

(She pulls him up.)

OWEN: But if I reach here, the ball goes there, Ruth, wherever I reach is where it won't be!

RUTH: That can't be true!

OWEN: *(Indicating his bloody nose.)* Look at me, Ruth, if anything's true, it's true, I know my own life —

RUTH: Put out your hands!

(She puts out his hands.)

RUTH: Now keep your eyes open, keep your eye on the ball, and catch it!

OWEN: OK, I'll try!

RUTH: Here it comes . . . here it comes . . . here it comes . . .

(Their eyes track the incoming ball. Owen's ready to catch it. Boom, it hits Owen in the face with a loud smack. He falls over, clutching his face in quiet agony. Ruth doesn't react in horror this time. She just looks down at him.)

RUTH: *(After a long beat.)* But see, aren't you glad you made the *effort?*

OWEN: *(From down on the ground, curled up in pain, after a beat.)* Yeah, I'm glad.

RUTH: You'll get the next one. Just tell yourself, "I'll get the next one."

OWEN: "I'll get the next one."

RUTH: You can't lose hope, Owen. That's what I tell the kids. We can't lose hope. It's all we've got.

(She sits down, eats some popcorn, watches the field with interest.)

RUTH: I really think we have a shot this year. I think we're really gonna go all the way.

(Loud crack of the bat hitting the ball.)

END OF PLAY

I Think You Think I Love You

KELLY YOUNGER

This play is dedicated to Maureen.

I Think You Think I Love You was originally developed as part of Ensemble Studio Theatre/LA Project's Winterfest (Isabel Storey, Elizabeth Logun, Jennifer Rowland, Producers.) on February 23, 2003, at Theatre/Theater in Hollywood. It was directed by Jenny O'Hara and the cast was as follows: Branwyn: Lizzie Peet; Mark: Jake Eberle. *I Think You Think I Love You* premiered on March 23, 2003 at the Ruskin Group Theatre in Los Angeles. It was directed by John Ruskin and the cast was as follows: Branwyn: Jennifer Palais; Mark: Chad Mokle

CHARACTERS
> BRANWYN
> MARK

SETTING
> A living room

AUTHOR'S NOTE
> Branwyn is pronounced *BRAN-win* with a hard *a* like in the word "grand." The director is encouraged to use as many props as makes the actress *uncomfortable* on stage (e.g., a canteen, hiking boots, bug spray, two urns, sunglasses, tree branches, and anything else one would take on a hike to spread the ashes of a mother and a cat). Spilling, dropping, tripping, and fumbling are all highly encouraged as long as it remains somewhat natural. The director may also wish to have the actress change costumes on stage (i.e., from dirty hiking clothes to regular clothes as long as it is done without nudity). Whatever choices are made, Branwyn should speak and move as quickly and frenetically as possible throughout the whole play while Mark should resemble a deer in headlights.

• • •

Branwyn enters, exhausted from a long hike, wearing an overstuffed backpack. She plops down on the chair, dropping the bag at her feet. Leaves fall from her hair and grass from her boots. She begins to unpack when there is a timid knock at the door. She rises and opens it to find Mark wearing a coat and tie.

MARK: Hi. I'm—
BRANWYN: Look. I'm not really in the mood, so let's make this quick.
MARK: (*Entering:*) Oh. Is this not —
BRANWYN: No, it's fine. I mean it's not, but it is. I just got back from kind of a hike. With my mother. Not *with* her, but with her, you know? Her ashes.
MARK: Oh?
BRANWYN: She died four months ago. No. Five. God has it already been five months? Yes. That's right.
MARK: I'm . . . so sorry.
BRANWYN: Why? Did you kill her?
MARK: What?! Oh my God, no! I meant—
BRANWYN: I know, I know. I'm just kidding. Like I said, I'm in a mood, you

know? But it's what she wanted. Not to die, of course, but to hike. Once it got her. Leukemia. That's what it ended up being, even though it didn't start out that way. I mean it did, of course. The doctor said leukemia first, and we we're all like — oh my God! — And she went through all this chemo, you know, a whole summer of it. And then the doctor couldn't find any trace of it. The leukemia. And we all started thinking, maybe she never had it to begin with, you know? Maybe they couldn't find any *(Using her fingers to make quotation marks.)* "trace of it" because it was maybe never there. That happens sometimes, you know, where they misdiagnose and of course there's no *(Using her fingers.)* "trace of it" . . . God, I swore I'd never be that annoying person who uses her hands to make *(Using her fingers.)* "bunny ears." But once we thought she maybe never had it, she up and dies. And after we had the bone marrow test and of course the only match is my sister who turned the whole thing into some conspiracy against her, you know, like of course *she* would be a match and I wouldn't because Mom and I we're always a better match and now the one time they get along it's because Mom wants to suck the marrow out of her bones — literally, you know — and by the time I convinced her to go through with it she was of course relieved to find out she did-n't have to do it, but then it turned out she *did* in fact have traces of it, it was just hiding. And of course it came out of hiding so quickly that it just jumped out and said, *(Using her fingers.)* "I'm back, I'm moving in, bought, sold and furnished, home sweet home" in my mother's body and then that was that.

MARK: Are you sure this isn't —

BRANWYN: An exaggeration? Are you kidding? That's nothing. My sister, after all this, crowns herself the *(Using her fingers.)* "keeper of the ashes." That's what she starts calling herself, the *(Using her fingers.)* "keeper of the ashes" as if she were some knight of the round table chivalrously guarding both sets of ashes.

MARK: Both?

BRANWYN: Her cat. Henry. The one that died three weeks before Mom died. She had it cremated too.

MARK: You can cremate a —

BRANWYN: You can cremate anything. But of course this cat Henry takes on epic proportions. It's no ordinary cat. No. It's Henry, this stray she found like ten years ago at work. A femur, or no, what's the word for a wild cat?

MARK: Feral?

BRANWYN: That's it. This feral cat that lives in the parking lot where her office is. She starts feeding this thing, and of course she has to name it and names it Henry, so she starts feeding this thing two, three times a day for about three years. But then when she gets transferred across town, she still goes back to feed it. Two, three times a day. Can you believe that? To leave on your lunch break and go feed a feral cat named Henry at your old job where they transferred you in the first place to get rid of you? And you keep coming back because Henry will supposedly starve to death if she doesn't feed it? And she does this for like another five years, sometimes even getting my mother to go do it when she had a meeting or something if you can believe it, until finally she decided to trap it in a cage. Then she brings Henry home to her apartment, which already has four cats living there — she's one of those women, you know? With a lot of cats? — But Henry of course flips out and the other cats flip out because he's feral and they're not, but then they start acting feral and peeing all over her carpet because they're mad that Lauren brought home this stray. And she has to keep Henry living in a cage, in her kitchen. She never lets the thing out? And she sees nothing wrong with this. So the whole apartment now stinks of cat urine but she thinks this is all in my head and that I'm criticizing her, which of course I am. Wouldn't you?

MARK: I'm more of a dog person myself, but I guess —

BRANWYN: But the best part is that when Henry dies — she still won't tell me how, I think the other cats got together and poisoned it — she decides to get him cremated. So that's why she's the *(Using her fingers.)* "most qualified" to be the *(Using her fingers.)* "keeper of the ashes" for Mom because she already has experience keeping the ashes of Henry. And here's where it gets weird.

MARK: Here?

BRANWYN: She starts having these tea parties and things. With Henry and Mom. I dropped by with a map to plan the hike with her and there she was, at the table, pouring imaginary tea in these little cups, to two urns. I mean one was a bigger urn, my mother's, but she also has this little five-pound marble box with Henry in it. And she's in full conversation. And of course I flip out and start laughing, not screaming, but laughing because the whole scene is so absurd, which of course causes her to flip out and start screaming. And that's when I find out Lauren's doing all these weird things with the ashes. I mean beyond the tea party. She's taking Henry and Mom with her on her errands, fastening their seat belts and everything, to the market, the dry cleaners. She sleeping with them. Can you believe that? I mean, look, I get it. They're both dead. I miss Mom too — not Henry — but I'm not going to sleep with her ashes. So I demand we do this hike like ASAP because that's what Mom wanted. To go to Castle Rock and spread her ashes. That's where we always went to girls' camp, even Mom when she was a girl, and that's where she wanted her ashes spread. It's this big rock some Indian maiden threw herself off of when she didn't see her hunky warrior coming back from the hunt, or something. But of course Lauren refuses to go hiking. She doesn't want Mom's ashes spread someplace that she can't go visit.

MARK: Why can't she —

BRANWYN: Exactly. Lauren is a wimp. Every year at camp we all had this amazing hike to Castle Rock, but Lauren would always chicken out saying, it's too far, I have blisters, I'm allergic to high altitude, whatever. So she's basically refusing not only to go on the hike but to give me Mom's ashes. And after going around and around for days she finally agrees to give 'em up but on one condition. (*She waits for Mark to ask.*)

MARK: Oh. Sorry. What condition?

BRANWYN: Henry. Uh-huh. can you believe it? She wants me to spread Henry's ashes with Mom's. That's what Mom would want, she says. She really believes Mom wants her ashes mixed in with some parking-lot cat named Henry. So I say, fine, thinking I just have to get Mom out of there and up to the mountains. And what was supposed to be this beautiful moment, two sisters, sad daughters, saying good-bye to their mother, together, has now turned into a solo hike with two urns on my back, one my mother, and one a cat.

MARK: I don't know what to say. That's awful?

BRANWYN: No. What's awful is what I did. Once I get all my gear on and am ready to go, I realize that extra five pounds, what's now Henry, is too much to carry. You know, break the camel's back and all. And so I decide there's no way I'm going to go through with it, and since there's no way Lauren will ever know, I just leave Henry in the car and start off with Mom. Just the two of us. And I hike and hike. Past the old girls' camp. Past the lake — the one where they filmed *Parent Trap*, remember that old movie with the twins and all the antics and confusion? Not the new one with that freakishly skinny girl, but the one from the '60s with that freakishly homely girl who looked like Anthony Michael Hall in *Breakfast Club* and the editing was so bad you could totally see the split screen trying to pretend that just that one kid was really a twin. Remember? (*Mark shakes his head, completely at a loss.*)

BRANWYN: Anyway, that's where they filmed it. So I keep hiking up toward Castle Rock. And it's perfectly clear, the day, you know? Really blue up there. You can look out and see the cloud layer, or I guess it's really the smog layer, hovering all over San Bernardino, but where I am, where we are, is fresh and dry and thin. And after about four hours — it used to only take three when I was a kid but that's because, actually, I don't know why that is, it just was — so I finally get there to this huge rock. It's like thirty feet up and there's this huge flat area on top where you can sit and look out over the whole mountain and Big Bear Lake and everything. And I do my thing, you know? What I set out to do.

(She pantomimes the actions.)

BRANWYN: I take out Mom's ashes. I recite a line from Shakespeare — *Othello*, she liked that play. Actually, no. I don't think she ever saw it. Or even read it. God what am I talking about? I've never read it. I searched and searched for the perfect poem or song or quotation or something to say at that moment, but I couldn't find anything, so I flipped open a book of Shakespeare plays — he's supposed to be the best, right? — and just dropped my finger down into a play and it was *Othello* so that's what I memorized and that's what I said. And then I said . . . good-bye Mom . . . and tossed her ashes up in the air. And by air, of course, I mean wind, and by wind I mean the wind blowing in the direction I'm standing and I'm sorry, but I never paid much attention to those old sailor movies that say never spit into the wind because sure enough Mom blows right out and back at me. And by back at me, of course, I mean my face and by my face I mean my nose and mouth. So of course my face is all wet and weepy so Mom sticks to my face, and I freak out and inhale with horror and down she goes. Not all of it, or her, but enough, you know? Just a bit to be absolutely horrified that I've just inhaled some of my mother, which I'm sure could be some beautiful metaphor for Mom living inside me and all that sentimental bull but really all I can think is my mother tastes like charcoal. Not that I know, but you can imagine, you know? So I start pouring water out of my canteen onto my face and into my mouth and nose and I'm stumbling all around the top of Castle Rock thinking I'm either going straight to hell for cannibalizing my mother or I'm going straight off the side of this rock like that old Indian girl who couldn't live without her lover. It's OK, you can laugh.

MARK: I wasn't going to —

BRANWYN: It's OK, really. Totally absurd day.

MARK: Wait. This all happened today?

BRANWYN: Yeah.

MARK: And you're sure you still want to . . . ?

BRANWYN: Wait. I forgot the cat.

MARK: The cat?

BRANWYN: This is the worst part.

MARK: It gets —

BRANWYN: It always gets worse, doesn't it? I just couldn't bear to mix Mom and Henry up together, no matter how much the cat meant to Lauren, even if Mom occasionally fed the damn thing. So when I got back to the car, I took Henry out of the glove compartment, that's where I put him, I was afraid the sun might shine through the car and burn him or something, which of course couldn't happen because he was in his marble box, and of course he was burnt already. So I took him out, walked across the road and dumped him near a tree. And then, here's the worst part, I took a picture of it, or him. All spread out there. But I had to get real close with the camera so Lauren wouldn't see the car in the background, or the road. I had to pretend that he was dumped right near the rock, which of course by now is a four-hour hike away, and nowhere near my mother's remains.

MARK: What are you going to tell her when you give her the picture?

BRANWYN: The truth, of course. That Mom and Henry are together forever, departed mother and feral cat, atop Castle Rock, Big Bear Mountain, California, United States of America.

(She sits, exhausted.)

BRANWYN: So. *(Indicating the house:)* What do you think?

MARK: *(Looking around:)* About what? the cat?

BRANWYN: No. The house.

MARK: Oh. *(Looking again:)* It's very nice.

BRANWYN: Rare 1930 Tudor-style, four bedrooms, three baths, formal living room, quaint dining room, large family room, remodeled kitchen with solid cherry shaker cabinets, upgrades include Anderson double pane wood windows, French doors, designer and faux paint, hardwood floors, all copper plumbing, forced air heat, large backyard with automatic sprinkler systems, and good school district. *(Using her fingers:)* "Lovers of vintage homes won't want to miss this one!"

MARK: I see.

BRANWYN: Do you want to take a look?

MARK: At what?

BRANWYN: The house.

MARK: Sure, I guess. Do you want me to?

BRANWYN: Well the sign does say, Do Not Disturb Occupant, but how else will you know?

MARK: Know what?

BRANWYN: If you want to buy it.

MARK: Your house?

BRANWYN: It's my mother's. I can't afford to keep it.

MARK: I already have a house. I mean a condo.

BRANWYN: Investment property then.

MARK: No, I live there.

BRANWYN: But you're looking for another one.

MARK: No.

BRANWYN: Oh, you're a realtor. Sorry. That makes sense. What's your client looking for, because to be honest, this place is a dump. The pipes aren't really copper, just painted that color, the fourth bedroom is really just a closet I squeezed an old futon into, and the school district is crap. Trust me. I went to school here.

MARK: I'm not a realtor. I own a used bookstore. Maybe I have the wrong address or something, I was . . . you're Branwyn, right?

BRANWYN: Yes. Winnie. I go by Winnie. *(Standing:)* Wait. Who are you?

MARK: Mark.

BRANWYN: Mark?

MARK: Yes. Mark. *(Pause; no recognition, deeply embarrassed:)* Patrick's friend? He's *(Using his fingers.)* "setting us up"?

BRANWYN: *(Quickly covering her mouth in a panic:)* Oh my God!

MARK: We were going to go to dinner and then that night of ten-minute plays or—

BRANWYN: Oh my God! Is that tonight?

MARK: I think so. *(Examining tickets from his pocket:)* I mean, I'm pretty sure. I got the tickets for tonight.

BRANWYN: I just made a complete . . . *(Shielding her eyes.)* oh my God, I can't even look at you.

MARK: *(Looking at his clothes:)* I know. I'm color blind and they don't make adult Garanimals.

BRANWYN: No no no, you look fine. You look *great*, but you have to go.

MARK: But I'd really like to —

BRANWYN: Go go *go*! You have to go, *now.*

MARK: Why?

BRANWYN: I'm too humiliated! Let's just pretend none of this ever—

MARK: But I can't go through all this again, it makes me too nervous, the dressing up, the talking, the —

BRANWYN: *(Still hiding her face:)* Please *please* just go, I'm so sorry, so sorry. God, Winnie, you're such a fool.

MARK: No you're not, not at all!

BRANWYN: *(Shuffling him to the door:)* Please *please*. Just go!

MARK: What about the tickets?

BRANWYN: Oh God don't say another word, I'm so embarrassed. Tell Patrick what a horrible, wretched, nut case I am and that you hate him forever even suggesting you take me out and that you'll never forgive him —

MARK: But I actually want —

BRANWYN: *(Pushing him out the door:)* No, no buts. Trust me, I'm doing you a favor, you want nothing to do with me.

MARK: Yes I —

(She slams the door on him, turns, leans her back on it and sighs, horrified. Long, humiliated pause.)

(There is a timid knock on the door.)

(Branwyn looks up, pauses, and turns to the door. She hesitates then opens it. Mark is standing there.)

MARK: *(Entering:)* Hello. I'm Mark. Patrick's friend?

(He extends his hand.)

MARK: I'd really like to take you to dinner.

(She hesitates, then takes it. He does not let go.)

BRANWYN: Branwyn. Call me Winnie.

MARK: I know. *(Beat.)* I've heard a lot about you.

END OF PLAY

PLAYS FOR
TWO WOMEN

Halasana

KAYLA S. CAGAN

CHARACTERS
HILLARY: Harriet's twin; mid-twenties
HARRIET: Hillary's twin; mid-twenties

TIME
Now

LOCATION
Hillary and Harriet's apartment living room. An American city.

•   •   •

Hillary and Harriet, fraternal twins, are in their post-college apartment, getting ready for Hillary's yoga exhibition. Well, Hillary is getting ready. Harriet is busy sucking down a bong hit. They are dry, funny women.

HARRIET: *(Inhaling an awesome amount from her bong, and exhaling the first line.)* My feet are never in the right position. I hate this shit.

HILLARY: It's good for you.

HARRIET: My feet hurt too much. My hamstrings are tight.

HILLARY: If you can't comfortably rest your feet on the floor in plow pose, you should use a chair.

HARRIET: Shut up.

HILLARY: Can't.

HARRIET: I hate everything.

HILLARY: You're awesome.

HARRIET: Nothing fits me. Why can't I be freakin' skinny?

HILLARY: Because God hates you.

HARRIET: Why are you my sister?

HILLARY: Because our parents hate you.
(Pause.)

HARRIET: So, I really have to go to this thing.

HILLARY: Yep. And you'll love it. You need to love it.

HARRIET: Don't tell me to/

HILLARY: /You need to/

HARRIET & HILLARY: Open my/your lotus heart

HARRIET: Again.

HILLARY: You close yourself off to/

HARRIET: Quiet, dude.

HILLARY: Aren't you at least happy for me?

HARRIET: Huh?

HILLARY: Happy. You know *HAPPY*, surely. Joyous, gay, blissful, exuberant.

HARRIET: Yeah. I'm happy for you. I'm *thrilled*. It's not every day your twin becomes a certified yogi.

HILLARY: You're right. It isn't. It's going to be a glorious ceremony and exhibition.

HARRIET: Rich is going to be there, isn't he?

HILLARY: I imagine so. He *is* my teacher.

HARRIET: And Mom and Dad.

HILLARY: They *are* invited.

HARRIET: Fantastic.

HILLARY: Fine, you don't have to be happy for me.

HARRIET: Thanks.

HILLARY: Heads up, Mike and Tommy will be there, too.

HARRIET: Is there going to be any guy there I haven't screwed? Unbelievable.

HILLARY: I can't stop you from —

HARRIET: Opening my lotus heart?

HILLARY: Maybe you should keep your inner smile close-lipped. *(She smiles at this. They both laugh at this. Harriet laughs more than Hillary.)* So, you're really not happy for me. I'm going to be fully certified. I'll be able to teach. I'll be able to pay my rent. And I'll be healthy.

HARRIET: Sure. I said I was happy earlier.

HILLARY: But you aren't.

HARRIET: Well, you'll just change, that's all.

HILLARY: Yes — it's called employment.

HARRIET: That's not what I mean.

HILLARY: I'll be exactly/

HARRIET: You'll change.

HILLARY: You're silly.

HARRIET: You'll be phony, like all of them.

HILLARY: What are you talking about?

HARRIET: *(Snickers.)*

HILLARY: Just say it.

HARRIET: You're never going to pound Cheetos with me again.

HILLARY: What?

HARRIET: You're going to be overtaken by the *appreciation* of your fucking poses, and I'll say, "Hey, Hill, how 'bout we go get stoned and throw back some Pop-Tarts" and you'll say shit like "Love to Harry, I mean Harriet, but my body is a temple and I'll only splurge on tofutti choc-o-mint bars, so go ahead and feed yourself without me. Rich and I, will be cleansing our souls on a meditation retreat in Sedona." Then where will I be? Man.

HILLARY: Let me get this straight. You're pissed at me, because I'm being certified to teach yoga, and I won't be able to eat Cheetos with you.

HARRIET: Not unless their organic.

HILLARY: I always knew you were a freak, because we shared the same brain and the same family and the same friends and the same schools and the same almost-everything. But you're losing me on this one, Harry. I was happy for you when you made all-star track. I was happy for you when you collected every scholarship possible in the country. I was there cheering you on at every turn and jump and leap and even when you/

HARRIET: When I broke my ankle/

HILLARY: I was there for you.

HARRIET: And I'm here for you.

HILLARY: You're madly disappointed that I am going to be certified. I didn't force you to come to class when I was a student, nor did I use you as a guinea pig when I started to intern and teach. So, you're just pissed that, I'm what, doing what?

HARRIET: You don't get it.

HILLARY: Then tell me. I'm not dense. I just have no fucking clue.

HARRIET: You should understand by now.

HILLARY: I'm not telepathic.

HARRIET: You're my twin.

HILLARY: And you're my twin. But you're fucking stumping me. Help me out here.

HARRIET: No.

HILLARY: No?

HARRIET: No.

HILLARY: Jesus Christ. I have to go. I have to get ready.

HARRIET: Then go.

HILLARY: What is the matter with you???

HARRIET: You are going to leave anyway, so you might as well start now.

HILLARY: *(Dawns on her.)*

HARRIET: *(Stares.)*

HILLARY: I'm doing something without you?

HARRIET: *(A pause.)* I don't care what you do.

HILLARY: Yeah. Yeah, you do. It's killing you.

HARRIET: Get over yourself.

HILLARY: We are out of college.

HARRIET: And?

HILLARY: And neither one of us have been able to get a decent job. So now, I'm finally doing something I like, something I literally fell into, and you can't stand it.

HARRIET: Nope.

HILLARY: Yep. That's what this whole damn attitude is about with you.

HARRIET: What?

HILLARY: Our positions . . .

HARRIET: It's a little soon to jump to conclusions, isn't it?

HILLARY: Well, isn't that what you're doing? You're the one predicting I will never eat another Cheeto again.

HARRIET: That's not it . . . You're missing it.

HILLARY: No, I'm not.

HARRIET: What?

HILLARY: That's why you are being a bitch about Mom and Dad being there, Rich and Mike and Tommy/

HARRIET: You love to rub it in that my relationships don't work out!

HILLARY: What relationships are you talking about? Your one-nightstands you chalk up to proposals? Harry, get over it. I'm not taking anything or anyone from you, I'm not changing your life for you at all.

HARRIET: You can't stand for anything good to happen to me. You're still gloating over my broken ankle.

HILLARY: Are you kidding me? Can you hear me in there? *(Indicating her head.)* You're a joker. You need to lay off the dope, yo.

HARRIET: OK, OK. Why else would you go into a purely physical occupation when you didn't even care about getting off the damn couch, like a couple of years ago?

HILLARY: First, of all it's not purely physical.

HARRIET: Fuh-uckkkk. I know you don't buy into all of that spiritual shit. You're too much like me.

HILLARY: Which is?

HARRIET: Truthful.

HILLARY: Union is truthful. Mental, physical, spiritual union is truthful.

HARRIET: And now you think you have that because you stretch your ass on a mat all day?

HILLARY: Should I only have a union with you then?

HARRIET: *(Silence, then, nodding.)* Yes.

HILLARY: Grow up.

HARRIET: You're being selfish.

HILLARY: I'm not.

HARRIET: Are too.

HILLARY: What do you want from me? I graduate today.

HARRIET: You know what you should do.

HILLARY: What?

HARRIET: You shouldn't go.

HILLARY: What?

HARRIET: If you really love me, you won't go.

HILLARY: Uh, what?

HARRIET: Don't pretend you don't know what I'm talking about.

HILLARY: I'm afraid I don't, Harry. You're really scaring me. You don't want me to graduate?

HARRIET: You can't do this to me.

HILLARY: Do what to you? I'm doing this for ME! So I can pay rent! So I can be happy! HOW IS THAT HURTING YOU?

HARRIET: It's hurting us!

HILLARY: No, honey, it's not/

HARRIET: You'll be going off and/

HILLARY: I'm going to be working and teaching at the studio in the freakin' burbs. I don't understand!

HARRIET: We won't live in the same world anymore.

(Pause.)

HILLARY: I never would have thought you would be so . . . self-centered.

HARRIET: You don't know what you are about to do to us.

HILLARY: I bend over backwards for you. Always have, always will.

HARRIET: You can't go through with this! Think about it!

HILLARY: I'm trying, and I just don't see what's wrong with it!

HARRIET: I'm not going.

HILLARY: Then, stay.

HARRIET: Think about what you are doing.

HILLARY: It's not even a big deal.

HARRIET: It's the biggest deal.

HILLARY: You're right. It is. I'm growing. I'm stretching. And you?

HARRIET: You're going to be late. Don't let me keep you.

HILLARY: I won't. Thanks for/

(As Hillary picks up her bag, yoga mat, etc. . . . and heads to the door, Harriet grabs her bong. Hillary slams the door.)

HARRIET: /Everything.

(Hillary fires up the bong again, inhales, and begins to deeply chant/exhale "Om.")

END OF PLAY

Woman of the Theatre

JULIE JENSEN

CHARACTERS
WENDY: early twenties
FLOATING PINATA HEAD: forties to fifties

SETTING
The lobby of an old theater

. . .

We're in the lobby of an old theater. Wendy, a young woman in her early twenties, is plain, unaffected, "with the personality of wall board," as her father says. She wears a tool belt and work boots. She's shoveling. [Note: All underscored lines are meant as narration.]

WENDY: Me and Lu, we used to date each other because no one else would have us. Anyway one summer Lu got a hair up his butt. He was gonna open up the old opera house and make a real theater out of it. "First you're gonna have to shovel the bat guano out of the lobby," I told him. And so that's what I was doing when in comes this woman. Flowing and flying. Her face to the wind. "Oh my God, oh my God, oh my God," she says.
(Floating Pinata Head enters, circles, and lands. She's a middle-aged woman with an overt theatricality.)
FLOATING PINATA HEAD: The weather out there is a positive fright!
WENDY: She looks like the hood ornament on a '58 Plymouth.
FLOATING PINATA HEAD: I look a mess. I feel a mess. What time is it?
WENDY: Ten after two.
FLOATING PINATA HEAD: Oh! The traffic from Chinchilla!
WENDY: This is Floating Pinata Head. That's what we named her. Left over from when she taught dancing. "Lead with your breast bone," she said. "Let your head float like a pinata."
FLOATING PINATA HEAD: You may call me Miss Head.
WENDY: Right. I saw you in *Macbeth.*
(Floating Pinata Head leaps up, jumps three times, and spits north.)
FLOATING PINATA HEAD: Never say the title of that play in the theater. It's bad luck. Say "The Scottish Play."
WENDY: Oh.
FLOATING PINATA HEAD: Now which version of "The Scottish Play" did you see?
WENDY: The one at the Chinchilla High School Multi-Purpose Room.

FLOATING PINATA HEAD: Ah, the children, the precious, precious children. There is nothing like an audience of children. They don't know a thing, cannot understand a word, and yet they are touched. They depart from the theater completely altered.

WENDY: <u>I'm looking at her mouth. It moves more than any other person's mouth.</u>

FLOATING PINATA HEAD: And you are?

WENDY: <u>She never could remember my name.</u> I'm Wendy Burger.

FLOATING PINATA HEAD: Unfortunate name. For an actress. But then you're not an actress.

WENDY: Well, no, not yet. But soon, I hope.

FLOATING PINATA HEAD: At this theater?

WENDY: My dad thinks it would be a good idea.

FLOATING PINATA HEAD: And are you auditioning?

WENDY: Well, yes. Yes, I am, I think. Maybe.

FLOATING PINATA HEAD: And what are you doing?

WENDY: Right now? Not much.

FLOATING PINATA HEAD: For your piece.

WENDY: For my audition piece?

FLOATING PINATA HEAD: For your audition piece.

WENDY: Well, I have a lot of things, actually . . . .

FLOATING PINATA HEAD: Narrow it down.

WENDY: Right. Well, my dad, he likes the singing and dancing. That's what gets people into the thee-ater, that's what he says.

FLOATING PINATA HEAD: It's theater, and your father is a cretin.

WENDY: Well, that ain't the first time he's been called that. I'll probably do something from Shakespeare.

FLOATING PINATA HEAD: Always a good choice. Would you like me to take a look at it?

WENDY: A look at it?

FLOATING PINATA HEAD: Yes. Give you some pointers.

WENDY: Right. Pointers.

FLOATING PINATA HEAD: I studied, of course, with the great Maud May Babcock.

WENDY: Right, the great Maud May.

FLOATING PINATA HEAD: And Maud May played here. She was in the original production of *Sturdy, Sturdy, Highland Lassie.*

WENDY: Right.

FLOATING PINATA HEAD: Well then, put down that wrench.

WENDY: <u>Before I know it, she's launched. And so am I.</u>

(Floating Pinata Head sets down her stuff and begins to applaud.)

FLOATING PINATA HEAD: I begin every session this way. You must learn to love that sound. The sound of the clap.

WENDY: Oh.

FLOATING PINATA HEAD: Well, then, let's begin. Give me the first line.

WENDY: "Out, out, brief . . . ."

FLOATING PINATA HEAD: Stop. Look at yourself.

WENDY: I just came from my job.

FLOATING PINATA HEAD: And you're an auto mechanic?

WENDY: No I drive a truck. UPS.

FLOATING PINATA HEAD: You're either a truck driver or an actress. What does an actress wear? Look at me. Ready for an audition at any moment, any time, anywhere. Here take this scarf, draw focus away from those boots. *(Wendy takes the scarf and drapes it backwards.)*

WENDY: Thank you.

(Floating Pinata Head eyes the effect, then she stares at Wendy's boots.)

FLOATING PINATA HEAD: Wait a minute. Do I know you?

WENDY: I took Hula from you in the third grade.

FLOATING PINATA HEAD: But of course, I never forget a face. You also wore boots back then, didn't you? Because your mother wore boots. After which she ran off with that strange woman schoolteacher from Chinchilla. All right, all right. Give me the first line.

WENDY: "Out, out . . .

FLOATING PINATA HEAD: Wait just a minute. That is a speech delivered by Macbeth.

(Wendy jumps up, twirls three times, and spits north.)

FLOATING PINATA HEAD: You may say the name of the character, not the name of the play.

WENDY: Oh.

FLOATING PINATA HEAD: But the character here is a man. A king.

WENDY: I know.

FLOATING PINATA HEAD: That forces credibility a bit, don't you think?

WENDY: I like what he has to say.

FLOATING PINATA HEAD: Ah, the magic of the poetry has captivated you. Well, we must always respect that. Go on.

WENDY: "Out, out, brief . . . ."

FLOATING PINATA HEAD: Stop! You must first enter.

WENDY: Enter, yes.

(Wendy goes over to the corner and walks to the center of the room.)

FLOATING PINATA HEAD: Do it again. Not as a truck driver this time, but as a monarch. The King. King hands. King feet. King head.

WENDY: Right.

FLOATING PINATA HEAD: But first, what is your reason for coming into the room?

WENDY: I want to blow out the candle.

FLOATING PINATA HEAD: Because the candle is life. It is light and it is life. You are drawn to it. Yet you are repelled by it. You want to live. You want to die. Yes! Let us see all that in your entrance.

(Wendy enters again.)

Now begin.

WENDY: "Out, out . . . ."

FLOATING PINATA HEAD: Not ow, ow, but ou*t*, ou*t*. Snapping *t*'s. Some of the most beautiful sounds in the English language. Snap those *t*'s whenever they occur.

WENDY: "Ou*t*, ou*t*, brief candle . . . ."

FLOATING PINATA HEAD: The word *brief.* What does that mean?

WENDY: Shor*t*.

FLOATING PINATA HEAD: Yes. And so we must color all words with their meaning.

WENDY: "Ou*t*, ou*t*, brief candle."

FLOATING PINATA HEAD: Go on.

WENDY: "Life's but a . . . ."

FLOATING PINATA HEAD: Life. Ah, life. The fullness, the joy, the power, the pain. Life in all its multiplicity. Life!

WENDY: *"Life's!"*

FLOATING PINATA HEAD: Yes! Go on.

WENDY: " . . . But a walking shadow."

FLOATING PINATA HEAD: Oh my, oh my, a walking shadow. What does that suggest?

WENDY: A shadow . . . that walks?

FLOATING PINATA HEAD: Yes! Try it.

WENDY: "Life's but a walking shadow."

FLOATING PINATA HEAD: Oh my, you are beginning to feel and, more importantly, to express. Go on. This is your baptism day.

WENDY: "A poor player . . . ."

FLOATING PINATA HEAD: Popping *p*'s. Popping *p*'s. Two in a row. What a *p*oet? And there's a third!

WENDY: "A *p*oor *p*layer that s*t*ruts and fre*t*s . . . ."

FLOATING PINATA HEAD: Oh, what glorious words: struts, frets. Let us see them.

WENDY: "A poor player that struts and frets . . . ."

FLOATING PINATA HEAD: Oh, yes, yes.

WENDY: "His hour upon the stage. And then . . ."

FLOATING PINATA HEAD: Ah, yes, and then . . . and then . . . listening, waiting, still with anticipation. And then—

WENDY: " . . . is heard no more."

FLOATING PINATA HEAD: Ah the tragedy of that, the poor player heard no more. All is silence. And then you flee, for you cannot bear it anymore. Oh, the flee, it is such a powerful exit, one of the finest.

WENDY: "And then is heard no more."

(She flees.)

FLOATING PINATA HEAD: That's good, it's grand. Now do you sense the power within you, the wonder, the glory?

WENDY: <u>I have no idea what she's talking about. But that ain't what I say. I say.</u> Yes. Oh, yes!

FLOATING PINATA HEAD: Good. Now give me back the scarf.

WENDY: Thank you. Thank you so much.

FLOATING PINATA HEAD: And don't let me see you in those boots again.

WENDY: Right.

FLOATING PINATA HEAD: And get the hair out of your eyes.

WENDY: Yes.

FLOATING PINATA HEAD: And put on a little makeup.

WENDY: Makeup?

FLOATING PINATA HEAD: Yes. This is the theater!

(Floating Pinata Head flees.)

WENDY: <u>And she's off like a fly from a crust of bread. And she has left behind a woman of the thee-ater.</u>

(She picks up her shovel, shoulders it, and walks with great dignity off the stage.)

END OF PLAY

Creatrix

DON NIGRO

CHARACTERS
TIFFANY
KIMBERLY

SETTING
A bedroom late at night. All we can see are Tiffany and Kimberly, two
teenage girls, sitting on the floor, in their pajamas, their backs up against
the end of a bed, staring downstage, bathed in the eerie light of an invisible television set in a darkened room.

• • •

*Tiffany and Kimberly, two teenage girls, sitting on the floor in their pajamas
in the dark, bathed in the eerie television light of a downstage TV set that is
invisible to us, as the tape they've been watching rewinds.*

TIFFANY: God, that was so awesome. I never get tired of watching it.

KIMBERLY: It's better than sex. Especially fellatio.

TIFFANY: Anything is better than fellatio.

KIMBERLY: How many times have we seen it?

TIFFANY: We've seen it a hundred and thirty-seven times. The movie. Not fellatio.

KIMBERLY: That many? Are you sure?

TIFFANY: I keep careful records of all significant world events in my diary.

KIMBERLY: This movie makes me happier than anything in the world.

TIFFANY: I know. It's like the first time you see it, you love it, but it puts you
off balance. You've got to see it again. Then the second time, you think
maybe you might get bored, but you realize there's things you missed that
you want to see again. And the third time you see it, it's like you get to
the other side of boredom, and start noticing all kinds of amazing details,
like the furniture and the plants and things going on in the background,
and you watch it again, and you watch it again, and it's like you're falling
deeper and deeper inside it, like down the rabbit hole. It's like astral pro-
jection, except it's better, because we can do it together. It's a country we
can visit on the same passport. It's like telepathy. Like the colors in my
head are in your head, too. It's this other world, and you can go there any
time you want, and nothing else is real. It's like going into the ocean, or
into the womb, or someplace you were before you were born, like there
are levels and levels of dreams, and you descend into the dreams, one
inside the other. And it's so real, after a while, it's like you suffer when

they suffer, but it's so beautiful, it fills you with this weird joy. After you watch it so many times, it feels like you made it yourself. You've become the creatrix.

KIMBERLY: The what?

TIFFANY: The creatrix. The goddess of all creation. It's like visiting the City of Lost Dreams in the middle of the Amazon jungle and scraping away an old vine from the pedestal of a statue and finding your own name written there and remembering suddenly that you're the one who built it.

KIMBERLY: Wow. That's deep. You're deep, Tiffany. You're so deep, my mother thinks you're a bad influence on me. She thinks you read too much to be a normal person. She's such a moron. Sometimes I just want to kill her.

TIFFANY: It doesn't matter what your stupid cow of a mother thinks. Nobody else exists. Our stupid parents don't exist, our stupid teachers don't exist. Nobody else can understand. It's pointless to even try to communicate with them because they're only listening with their ears. They'd think we were possessed by demons or something. They'd burn us for witches if we tried to explain the beautiful fog we live in when we watch this movie. This movie is like a big house you can wander in forever. It's like a memory theater, where each scene is a room, like the haunted castle where the gods live, where unspeakable acts are performed, over and over, like beautiful naked rituals. It's like the place you see when you look in the mirror in my stepfather's house in the room where the mirrors reflect each other from opposite walls, so that you can see rooms that open up into other rooms forever. It's more real than copulation because it includes copulation. It includes everything. Sometimes I see it when I close my eyes, just before I go to sleep, and it gets all mixed in with dreams. Like last night, I dreamed I was swimming naked in a pond, by my stepfather's house, and there was a hurdy-gurdy playing, and a crocodile swam up and ate me.

KIMBERLY: Gross.

TIFFANY: No. A certain amount of suffering is necessary for your art. Your own suffering, and sometimes the suffering of others. It's like being Vivienne.

KIMBERLY: Who?

TIFFANY: The girl in that poem we read in English class. Merlin is an older man who desires her, and he knows she's hungry for knowledge, and she cleverly persuades him to reveal to her, one by one, all his secret magical powers and spells, and then uses them to trap him inside a tree trunk forever. It's like that.

KIMBERLY: How is it like that?

TIFFANY: Because the movie is like a secret formula or spell that gives us power over them.

KIMBERLY: Over who?

TIFFANY: Over all of them. All the ones who want to order us around, tell us we can't see each other any more, put vile objects in our mouths and make us do unspeakable things. It gives us the power to do unspeakable things to them.

KIMBERLY: How does it do that?

TIFFANY: Because every time we watch it, we grow stronger.

KIMBERLY: I do feel stronger.

TIFFANY: What we need to do now is, we need to become them. We need to become those girls in the movie.

KIMBERLY: Do you mean the actresses? Or the characters they play? Or the people the characters were based on?

TIFFANY: Yes. All of the above. I want to enter the Fourth World, like Juliet and Melanie, and sleep with James Mason and Mario Lanza and Orson Welles.

KIMBERLY: Except of course they're all dead.

TIFFANY: Not in the movies.

KIMBERLY: But we're not in the movies.

TIFFANY: We could be.

KIMBERLY: That's unlikely.

TIFFANY: All the best things that could happen are unlikely. Love is very unlikely. I mean really intense, deep, supernatural love, which is a reality that's experienced in a part of the brain that most people don't even know they've got. But we know it. You and me. Just like the girls in the movie. Let's be them. I'll be Juliet.

KIMBERLY: You always get to be Juliet.

TIFFANY: Because I am Juliet. My father is a rectum who designs nuclear bombs. I have come to New Zealand to recover from life-threatening respiratory ailments. I have on more than one occasion seen the face of death.

KIMBERLY: So have I. I have infected bones in my legs. My pus must be drained with great regularity. It's made me delicate. But secretly I'm strong. Stronger than anybody could possibly imagine, just looking at me.

TIFFANY: Once I was shanghaied to the Bahamas, where the natives observed me unclothed. I was deeply traumatized. And then, every night, in my childhood, the bombs fell on London. Plus my mother is fucking somebody on the side.

KIMBERLY: Actually, that's my mother, in real life.

TIFFANY: It's everybody's mother, Kimmy. Life is tragic for a woman.

KIMBERLY: But on the bright side, you live in a magic castle.

TIFFANY: Yes, but all castles are infested with rats. A large rat comes into my room in the night and does unspeakable things. And my mother knows, and looks the other way.

KIMBERLY: I wish I could leave my family and be your sister. My father sells fish. Mother takes in boarders. They observe me unclothed through keyholes. I have been violated by the young boarder. His penis is a deeply unsavory instrument.

TIFFANY: To console ourselves, we take baths together, then curl up in bed like cats. I love to watch you fall asleep. You make noises like puppies.

KIMBERLY: Years later, when our astonishing Victorian mystery novels are published, we'll become very famous, move to Scotland and have intercourse with Mario Lanza. Me first.

TIFFANY: Both at the same time.

KIMBERLY: But what if Mario Lanza is already engaged to some stupendously gorgeous movie starlet with ostentatious bezongas?

TIFFANY: If he is, then we'll be morally obligated to kill her. We'll strangle her naked in her bath, in a scene worthy of Hitchcock and DePalma. For the greater good of humanity. For art's sake. With Mario Lanza singing *Pagliacci* in the background.

KIMBERLY: He's so dreamy. He's my chocolate soldier.

TIFFANY: When my parents threaten to take me back to London, my near-fatal respiratory illness returns. You never leave my bedside.

KIMBERLY: I'm loyal unto death.

TIFFANY: We write passionate letters that Orson Welles will publish when we're dead.

KIMBERLY: Then you find your mother in bed with a stranger.

TIFFANY: They're drinking tea, naked except for the whipped cream on her nipples, and on the end of his penis. Hello, I comment, cleverly.

KIMBERLY: Then you begin to giggle uncontrollably.

TIFFANY: [I] suppose you will now require some sort of explanation, says Mummy, wearily, like Tallulah Bankhead at the gynecologist. But I require no explanations. Sophisticated beyond my years, I have learned that all explanations are lies.

KIMBERLY: We're in love, she says.

TIFFANY: But what about father, I say?

KIMBERLY: He knows all about it. We'll all live together like civilized people.

TIFFANY: Oh, no, not that. Not civilized people. The most unspeakable crimes on the face of the earth are committed by civilized people. We much prefer the primitive races, because the savage mind is closer to the sensibility of the true artist.

KIMBERLY: So they conspire to send you to South Africa, to be trampled by ostriches.

TIFFANY: Life would be so much simpler if our mothers were dead.

KIMBERLY: Do you mean in the movie, or in real life?

TIFFANY: What's the difference?

KIMBERLY: If my mother knew I was letting you crawl in my window late at night and watch videos with me, she'd give birth to goats. She thinks you're mentally disturbed.

TIFFANY: In real life, or in the movie?

KIMBERLY: Both.

TIFFANY: Why couldn't your mother just die? People die every day. Why couldn't she?

KIMBERLY: Because what you want to happen never does.

TIFFANY: It does in the movie. Statues come alive and talk, and four-foot butterflies suck honey from gigantic flowers, and we do a three-way with Mario Lanza, who sings *Pagliacci* when he ejaculates.

KIMBERLY: In the movies, maybe. But not in Ohio.

TIFFANY: Why not in Ohio? How could we kill her? Let us count the ways. We could beat her over the head with a sand bag.

KIMBERLY: Or a brick. We could put a brick in a stocking.

TIFFANY: We'll invite her to tea, then lure her out to the park. I'll drop a pink stone along the pathway. Your mother will stop to pick it up. This will be the signal for you to commence whacking her violently over the head.

KIMBERLY: It's the day of the happy event. What fun. We had a jolly lunch at home, then took Mummy to tea, after which we bludgeoned her to death on the footpath. It was rather more difficult to do than I'd expected. I was hitting her and hitting her for quite a long time, until the brick came through the stocking. There was ever so much blood. But once having struck the first blow, a girl must keep going.

TIFFANY: [I] helped.

KIMBERLY: You were very helpful. My arms were getting tired.

TIFFANY: We struck her a total of forty-five times. I keep careful records in my diary.

KIMBERLY: It's such a beautiful story.

TIFFANY: [Let]'s do it.

KIMBERLY: We just did.

TIFFANY: No, but I mean, for real. Let's do it for real. Let's kill your mother.

KIMBERLY: We can't kill my mother.

TIFFANY: Why not? They did in the movie.

KIMBERLY: But that's a movie.

TIFFANY: But it's based on actual events. A movie is also real. At the still point of the turning world, art and life become one. My stepfather's an artist. He taught me. Art explains the world to us. It is immensely valuable that way. Art provides moral instruction. We can create a world and then live in it. We can force upon circumstance our own reality. You are the carnival queen and she is the property horse, and it's high time the old nag went to the glue factory. We can become our own movie. All that's needed is the one bold act to pierce the veil. It's the triumph of art.

KIMBERLY: But it wouldn't be the same.

TIFFANY: I don't see why not. We know how to do it. We've seen it a hundred and thirty-seven times. Only the perception of the observer changes. The movie itself is eternal. Make your life a movie. Be the director. Choose your reality.

KIMBERLY: But there wouldn't be talking statuary and giant butterflies.

TIFFANY: Why not?

KIMBERLY: Because those things don't really exist.

TIFFANY: They do if we have good special-effects people. Art is what enables a person to become one with the great universal creatrix. The goddess of all creation. Come on, Kimmy. Let's kill your mother. It'll make such a wonderful movie. We'll win Oscars. I've already prepared my acceptance speech.

KIMBERLY: You really are insane, you know?

TIFFANY: All great art springs from frustrated love, and what is love but the madness of desperation? We'll fashion a masterpiece from our mutual love. We will enter into the ecstasy of the animals, the pure, naked joy of creation. What do you say?

(Pause. They look at each other.)

KIMBERLY: Would I get top billing?

TIFFANY: Our people can negotiate all that.

KIMBERLY: Would I get to sleep with Mario Lanza?

TIFFANY: Unless you'd prefer Orson Welles.

(Pause.)

KIMBERLY: You're serious.

TIFFANY: Art is a very serious business.

(Pause.)

KIMBERLY: I think a person would need to believe very much, to make such a movie.

TIFFANY: People believe. They'll believe anything. They pray to a loving God who sends infants to hell and allows fathers to molest their children. We can make up a better religion than that. We can transform ourselves into the goddess. Put your hand on my heart.

(She takes Kimberly's hand and puts it on her heart. Then she puts her own hand on Kimberly's heart.)

Can you feel it? Can't you feel the great creatrix of the universe throbbing and seething and writhing beneath our flesh? She's dying to get out. It's our duty to release her. Are you with me? Because if you're not with me, nobody is.

(Pause. They look at each other.)

KIMBERLY: Where can we get a brick?

(They look at each other. The light fades on them and goes out.)

END OF PLAY

Different

LISA SOLAND

Different was first produced in 2005 as part of The Best of the Rest Fest at
The Actors Theatre in Santa Cruz, California, and was a finalist for the
2005 Kernodle New Play Competition in Fayetteville, Arkansas.

CHARACTERS

SUSAN: A woman in her early twenties. Self-absorbed and sexually propelled.

CHRIS: A conservative woman in her early twenties, with values and self-control.

SCENE

A small warm-up area in a gym

TIME

Now

• • •

Setting: A small, warm-up area in a gym. Perhaps there are some free weights scattered about and a floor mat or two. At Rise: Chris is alone, stretching.

SUSAN: *(Entering and seeing Chris alone.)* Can I ask you something?

CHRIS: OK.

SUSAN: Why don't you like me?

CHRIS: Why do you ask?

SUSAN: Some days you come in here and you almost, sort of talk to me, but I can tell you don't want to and then other days you do your best to avoid me all together. And since I seem to be here a lot of the times you come in, I'd kind a like to know why, so I don't have to feel this weird feeling every time I see you.

CHRIS: That's why you want to know, so *you* don't have to feel this weird feeling every time you see me?

SUSAN: That's right.

CHRIS: Why don't you just make up your mind to not worry about it?

SUSAN: Because it bothers me that you don't like me. It bothers me.

CHRIS: There are plenty of other people here who do. Why don't you just put your focus on them?

SUSAN: Why don't you want to tell me why?

CHRIS: Because that's not a fun game for me.

SUSAN: What do you mean?

CHRIS: *(Taking a breath.)* What usually happens when I try to explain to someone why I don't like him or her is that they get defensive. They try to explain to me how I have misread them so. And then I have to sit there and do my best to look like I'm listening. To look like I'm listening to them tell me how wrong I am. It's not fun. I hate listening to people defend themselves.

SUSAN: Maybe they're just trying to explain to you another point of view.

CHRIS: Yes, I guess you could say that. I wouldn't say it that way, but I guess you could.

SUSAN: What did I do? Just tell me what I did?

CHRIS: You know, sometimes people just don't like each other. There doesn't have to be a reason. There are plenty of people I don't like for no real reason other than we're . . . different from each other. And there's nothing wrong with that, right? Being different?

SUSAN: One wouldn't think so.

CHRIS: Let's just leave it at that.

SUSAN: Well, if you don't want to tell me why you don't like me, I'm certainly not going to twist your arm.

(Pause.)

I've noticed that you've gotten really tight in through here. Have you been working on your stomach area or . . . ? Because you look slimmer. You look great. Really great.

(No reply.)

SUSAN: *(Continued.)* Were you *trying* to lose weight or . . . ?

CHRIS: What are you doing?

SUSAN: I'm asking you a question.

CHRIS: Leave me alone.

SUSAN: You're a bitch.

CHRIS: Now comes the name calling.

SUSAN: You deserve it.

CHRIS: No, I don't. I have a right to not like you. I'm honest. You asked me and I told you. Why does that make me a bitch?

SUSAN: You don't even want to try to be friends.

CHRIS: That's right. I'll be friendly to you, but not friends.

SUSAN: "Friendly?"

CHRIS: Yes, friendly. That means we nod to each other. We smile. And when we have to, we exchange pleasantries about the weather — friendly.

SUSAN: But not friends.

CHRIS: That's right.

SUSAN: Why?

CHRIS: What is up with you today?

SUSAN: I'm just curious.

CHRIS: Number one, as I've been trying to explain, I don't like you. Number two, I have enough friends.

SUSAN: Enough friends? Is that possible — to have enough friends?

CHRIS: For me it is, yes.

SUSAN: Whatever happened to that saying by Walter Brennan, "I've never met a man I didn't like."

CHRIS: Will Rogers.

SUSAN: What?

CHRIS: Nothing.

SUSAN: One should never have enough friends.

CHRIS: Why does that make you uncomfortable, that I have enough?

SUSAN: It doesn't make me uncomfortable.

CHRIS: And because of a few catchy sayings by famous people, suddenly you have to live up to them and overextend yourself.

SUSAN: They're good sayings and they offer much value to my life.

CHRIS: Good, I'm happy for you.

SUSAN: You must be a very unhappy person.

CHRIS: Personal attacks. Let me look at my watch here. Four minutes into the answering of the question comes the personal attacks. Usually they come before the name calling. You seem to be out of order.

SUSAN: Listen, I'm just saying that you probably live a lonely life having that attitude about friends. I had a party Saturday night and there were so many people there that the neighbors called the cops. Not 'cause we were causing trouble or anything. It was just because there were so many people packed onto the front lawn that they started to pour out into the street, so some asshole called the cops.

(Beat.)

If you and I got along a little better than we do, I would have invited you too. We've got a pool and a Jacuzzi. You could have met someone there.

CHRIS: In the Jacuzzi?

SUSAN: Sure. I noticed you work out alone.

CHRIS: God, I'm so glad I studied this sort of thing. Had I run up against you a few years ago, you could have really screwed with my head.

SUSAN: OK. I get it. There's nothing I can do. You are just immovable. I guess there are some people who aren't going to like you, no matter what you do. I guess we just have to leave it at that.

CHRIS: Great.

SUSAN: Have a good workout.

CHRIS: Nice weather we're having.

SUSAN: Fuck you.

CHRIS: No thanks, you're not my type.

SUSAN: Oh, that's it. You're gay! Ah! I should have guessed that from the beginning. You're gay.

CHRIS: You know, I'm actually surprised that it took you till now to try that one. You're not as good as I thought.

SUSAN: *(Ignoring her, she continues to press.)* What is it you like about women?

CHRIS: Well, the women I like have restraint. Do you know what that is?

SUSAN: Yes, self-control.

CHRIS: Yes, that's right. Self-control.

SUSAN: *(Enticingly.)* I had an . . . experience once, with a woman.

CHRIS: *(Rises to exit.)* Excuse me.

SUSAN: Wait. What? What did I do? Please wait. Chris, right? Your name's Chris. Please. Just sit and talk to me. Please.

(Genuinely, or as genuine as possible.)

How is someone like me ever going to grow, if someone like you doesn't help?

(Chris stops.)

SUSAN: *(Continued.)* Please. Just talk to me.

CHRIS: *(Correcting Susan.)* With you.

SUSAN: *With* me. Whatever. Don't go. No one like you ever talks to me.

CHRIS: "Like me?" What do you mean, "like me"?

SUSAN: You're . . . I don't know. Strong.

CHRIS: Strong?

SUSAN: Yeah, strong. And smart — you seem to know a bunch of things, I don't. About stuff like . . . types of people and things. Smart. I'll bet you never let anyone hurt you.

CHRIS: *(An aside, from a calloused, hurting heart.)* Well, I don't know about that.

SUSAN: And I know I'm a . . . "type of person," but God, how am I ever going to change? How do I stand a chance to grow and learn about things if people like you don't try to help me?

CHRIS: *(A chord of compassion has been struck. She returns.)* OK. What do you want?

SUSAN: I want to know what it is about me you don't like.

CHRIS: *(Nice and gentle.)* Are you familiar with the word *narcissist?*

SUSAN: Narcissist. I've heard of it, yes. It's like . . . to be in love with yourself.

CHRIS: Yes, pretty much.

SUSAN: What does that have to do with me?

CHRIS: Well, let's not get too far ahead of ourselves, now.

(Gently, she continues.)

The word *narcissist* comes from Narcissus who was this Greek kid who basically falls in love with his reflection in a pool.

SUSAN: *(Suddenly remembering something very important.)* Oh, that reminds me. Hold on one second. I've got to make one quick call to our . . .

(She dials her cell phone.)

Hold on. Just a quick . . .

(Into phone.)

Johnny! Johnny, listen. There is a gold bracelet at the bottom of the pool.

(Beat.)

It's mine from Saturday night.

(Beat.)

When you clean the pool this afternoon, could you just get it out for me? It's worth a ton of money.

(Beat.)

Oh. Well, can you come back again, later today?

(Beat.)

Well, it was there. I saw it there this morning. Listen, where are you now? Oh, great — why don't you just swing back over on your way home?

(Beat.)

Yes, it's important. OK, great. It's in the deep end.

CHRIS: *(To self.)* The deep end.

SUSAN: *(Into phone.)* Great. Just scoop it out and leave it on the back porch.

(Beat.)

It's gold, yeah. Leave it on the back porch. Gold! You know, yellow.

CHRIS: *(To self.)* Yellow.

SUSAN: Thanks, Johnny. You're a sweetheart.

(She hangs up. To Chris.)

Now where were we?

CHRIS: You do know, don't you, that Johnny is going to steal your gold bracelet?

SUSAN: See? It's things like that. You know things about types of people and I want you to teach me. I mean, I don't believe you about Johnny because he's not only my pool man . . .

(Whispering.)

I've been seeing him.

CHRIS: Screwing him.

SUSAN: What?

CHRIS: Screwing him, right?

SUSAN: I don't know how to take you . . . to laugh or to be offended.

CHRIS: You want to know what I think?

SUSAN: *(After a brief moment of thinking.)* Yes, I do.

CHRIS: You better beat him to your house if you want that bracelet. Because if you don't get there in time, he'll say that he looked for it but couldn't find it. And if you stop to think about it, there's probably been other things missing from the around the house, right?

(Beat.)

SUSAN: OK, OK. I'm going. One thing at a time.

(Turns to go.)

I've got to clock out first. I'll talk with you later, Chris. 'Kay?

(Beat.)

'Kay?

CHRIS: Sure. Sure. Later.

(Susan exits.)

CHRIS: *(Continued.) (She takes her cell phone out of her purse and dials.)* Hey, Johnny. We still on for lunch?

(Pause as she listens to the excuse.)

Oh, I see. No, no, I understand. "When it comes to pools, Johnny's no fool." Not a problem. Business comes first.

(Beat.)

Sure, that sounds fine.

(Beat.)

Hey, will you do me a favor? Leave her gold bracelet on the back porch, Johnny. Leave it there.

(Lights out.)

END OF PLAY

Dance

GREG ZITTEL

Dance was first directed by David Roth at Cincinnati's Performing Arts School, with Audrey McLain as Sheilla and Jessica Levey as Jayna.

CHARACTERS
SHEILLA: teen
JAYNA: teen

SETTING
Sheilla's bedroom

• • •

Ohio. Early in the school year. Two teens in Sheilla's bedroom, books on the bed. Jayna sits, she has dark hair. An excited Sheilla gestures her way around the room. To look at Jayna is to see a lovely girl. To look at Sheilla is to see a young girl who is certain she is glorious. She wears styled clothes, earrings, and occasionally checks her manicured nails. She is fixing her ponytail.

SHEILLA: Don't be stupid.

JAYNA: *(Smiles.)* I'm not stupid.

SHEILLA: Eloise didn't listen to me and look what happened to her.

JAYNA: What happened to Eloise?

SHEILLA: She got fat. *(Laughs.)*

JAYNA: Nice.

SHEILLA: You could use a salad.

JAYNA: I came here to help you.

SHEILLA: I'm gonna get him.

JAYNA: I know it and you know it, but he doesn't know it.

SHEILLA: He'll know it.

JAYNA: If you'd just chill maybe we could concentrate and work on this.

SHEILLA: I can concentrate.

JAYNA: You're a wreck.

SHEILLA: I am a type "A" teen, I have nothing wrong with me, I am into power hysterics, and I exaggerate. That's no big deal. I am exactly the way a top teen beauty is supposed to be.

JAYNA: You don't see a problem there?

SHEILLA: Don't be an idiot. I am what a teen is. Believe me, I have no illusions of tender.

JAYNA: I believe you.

SHEILLA: I am at the hormonal peak of my existence and I need him.

JAYNA: You probably will get him.

SHEILLA: Ever since he came to the school I haven't been able to see straight.

JAYNA: He is a fox.

SHEILLA: Better looking than God.

JAYNA: Have you seen God?

SHEILLA: Don't be a jerk.

JAYNA: He's good-looking, but compare him to what you know.

SHEILLA: He's quiet, he keeps to himself.

JAYNA: Girls are afraid of him.

SHEILLA: I'm not.

JAYNA: He got an "A" on a paper in American History.

SHEILLA: When he took his first jump shot against Highway Christian I almost fainted.

JAYNA: How did you find out he was in Spanish Club?

SHEILLA: I saw him go around the corner on the second floor and followed him. There were six idiots talking about Spanish.

JAYNA: You listened?

SHEILLA: Sure. They were all dorks and there was the Spanish estooders, estu-piders, or something on a banner across the chalkboard.

JAYNA: Estudiantes?

SHEILLA: Maybe that was it. What does it mean?

JAYNA: *(Rolls her eyes.)* Astounding.

SHEILLA: He was so above them, they were all brains, unpopular, in need of germatoligists.

JAYNA: You mean skin doctors.

SHEILLA: *(Shocked at being corrected.)* That is what I said.

JAYNA: *(Nods.)* What was he doing?

SHEILLA: *(Gives Jayna a look.)* I just told you, are you dumb?

JAYNA: According to you I am, but I'm the one who knows how to speak Span-ish and you're the one who wants to learn.

SHEILLA: Stop. It's a minority language. Why should I know a minority lan-guage?

JAYNA: Because you want to get him?

SHEILLA: Correct. And I'm gonna get him. Face it, he's new, he doesn't know about me, my charms, my drive . . .

JAYNA: Your fangs.

SHEILLA: Get out. You're jealous. He's gorgeous, you have no chance, I'm hot and he's mine as soon as I let him know.

JAYNA: I admire your confidence.

SHEILLA: *(Looks in the mirror.)* You couldn't have what I have because you don't have what I have.

JAYNA: That's true.

SHEILLA: But you're nice, don't get me wrong. There's someone out there for you, someday, when your skin clears up or you lose ten pounds, but you'll never be me.

JAYNA: I'll never be you.

SHEILLA: No, let's be real, we're not supposed to be alike. There's supposed to be differences, there's supposed to be number ones.

JAYNA: And number twos.

SHEILLA: Oh honey I don't think you're a two yet, but if you listen to me you might get there?

JAYNA: *(Changes the subject.)* How do you know what he's like?

SHEILLA: Oh my God, just look at him.

JAYNA: He's from Mexico City, his father is a surgeon who just began at County Hospital.

SHEILLA: They must have money, that can't hurt.

JAYNA: He looks quiet.

SHEILLA: There is no problem here. I know he's Mexican, I know that, but his father's rich, not all Mexican's are illegal.

JAYNA: No, not all.

SHEILLA: And Jayna, this may be news to you but the world is changing. It is hip to be multi-culti.

JAYNA: Yes, but not too multi-culti right?

SHEILLA: That's right, you have to be careful on that one. Too multi-culti and it can be icky.

JAYNA: *(Shakes her head.)* I'll remember that.

SHEILLA: One look from me and he'll know his time has come.

JAYNA: Are you gonna look at him in Spanish too?

SHEILLA: I mean any girl would want him and at this time in my life I have to take a stand, I have to have the best-looking guy carrying my books, calling me on my cell phone . . .

JAYNA: Taking you out for guacamoles after a movie with subtitles.

SHEILLA: You're talking like such a jerk.

JAYNA: Maybe he'll ask you to the fall dance.

SHEILLA: Once he hears me speak and knows what I want him to know he'll ask me.

JAYNA: *(Does a couple easy moves.)* The salsa is easy, *marimba es fácil tambien.*

SHEILLA: He's not going to do those dances.

JAYNA: How do you know?

SHEILLA: *(Worried.)* What makes you think he will?

JAYNA: Mexico City?

SHEILLA: That doesn't mean he's a foreigner?

JAYNA: Hello?

SHEILLA: He came here, he wants to be American, he's got Major Motion Picture looks, you're making him sound like he's some hoochi-coochi cable TV type.

JAYNA: I'm just saying you might be making generalizations.

SHEILLA: You're making him sound migrant.

JAYNA: I'm just saying he might not act like we do here.

SHEILLA: Why do you think he came here?

JAYNA: I told you, his father, the hospital.

SHEILLA: That's his father that's not him.

JAYNA: OK. Why did he come here?

SHEILLA: To fall in love with me. Why else?

JAYNA: I think we should get started.

SHEILLA: How did you learn it?

JAYNA: What?

SHEILLA: This minority language you ditz.

JAYNA: My parents always wanted us to speak more than one language.

SHEILLA: That's so strange.

JAYNA: You think so?

SHEILLA: Of course it is.

JAYNA: OK, if you say so.

SHEILLA: American is hard enough, I have to take a language next year. I was thinking French, it's sexy but after I work with you and if it goes well with him, I may switch to Spanish.

JAYNA: I know "bi" families.

SHEILLA: Rosie has a family and she's "bi."

JAYNA: Bilingual.

SHEILLA: So what do we do first?

JAYNA: And I don't think Rosie is "bi," I think she is all the way, one way.

SHEILLA: Yeah, the wrong way, duh.

JAYNA: *(Opens a book, and shows it to Sheilla.)* In Spanish the subject and the verb are all in the one word.

SHEILLA: I know what they are.

JAYNA: A subject and a verb?

SHEILLA: Yeah. A subject is the person who does something and the verb is what is done.

JAYNA: OK, good. So in English we say "I go to the store."

SHEILLA: No problemo. Pretty good huh?

(Jayna shrugs her shoulders.)

SHEILLA: OK, this is serious, I know. So the subject is *I* and the verb is "went to the store."

JAYNA: Well the subject is *I* but the verb is *go*. The store is the object but we don't wanna mess with the object yet.

SHEILLA: I went to the store. *I* is the subject and *went* is the verb and forget about "to the store."

JAYNA: Yeah, but there's the tense. You're saying "went" and I'm saying "go."

SHEILLA: As long as we get there, who cares?

JAYNA: I'm saying "I go to the store," and you're saying "I went to the store."

SHEILLA: Well you're wrong, you don't say "I go to the store." You say, "I went to the store." Nobody says "I go to the store."

JAYNA: I'm trying to make a point about tense.

SHEILLA: You're making me tense.

JAYNA: I'm trying to teach you about Spanish.

SHEILLA: I'm trying to learn how to speak, not pass a test.

JAYNA: What do you want to say?

SHEILLA: *(Paints a picture.)* Well, there he'll be, in the Spanish Club and I'll lean over and say, "Hi, I haven't met you." *(She gives a "sexy" look.)* Then he'll say his name, and then I'll say my name.

JAYNA: OK, you would say, *"Hola, creo que todavía no nos conocemos."*

SHEILLA: *"Hola, yo no"* what?

JAYNA: *(Slow.)* *"Hola, creo que no nos conocemos."*

SHEILLA: "Hola," what's the rest?

JAYNA: *"Creo que todavía . . ."*

SHEILLA: *(Cutting her off.)* What am I saying?

JAYNA: *(Writing it down as she speaks.)* "Hello, I believe we haven't met yet."

SHEILLA: *(Takes the card.)* OK, I can say that. *(Reads.)* *"Hola, creo que todavía no nos conocemos."*

JAYNA: *Bueno.*

SHEILLA: And then I say what?

JAYNA: If you can get that far it'll be enough. Let him talk. Just say your name. You say, *me llamo* Sheilla.

SHEILLA: Stupid Spanish it's ridiculous what a girl won't do to get a guy you know?

JAYNA: Speaking Spanish isn't a bad idea. Maybe you should take it.

SHEILLA: I don't know. It would be a lot of work for just one foreigner. On the other hand there aren't a lot of guys like him, you know, ones that aren't greasy, who speak Spanish.

JAYNA: Sheilla, Sheilla, Sheilla. *(Astounded.)*

SHEILLA: Jayna honey, the point is to get out of the ghetto, not learn how to get in it. Spanish is too ghetto.
(Jayna smiles.)

(The phone rings. Sheilla answers.)

SHEILLA: Hello . . . Hi . . . Yes, she's here, she's been helping me with my Spanish . . . OK bye. *(Hands the phone to Jayna.)*

JAYNA: *(In perfect Spanish.)* Hola papá . . . Sí, hemos estado trabajando. Pronto estaré en casa . . . No, no tienes que recogerme . . . Yo voy a ir caminando para allá. Nos vemos al rato. Adiós.

(Translation: Hi Dad. Yeah, we've been working. I'll be home soon. No you don't have to pick me up. I'll walk. OK, see you soon. Good bye.)

(Jayna hangs up the phone and the two girls look at each other. Sheilla's mouth is open . . .)

JAYNA: I have to go.

SHEILLA: Who was that?

JAYNA: Dad.

SHEILLA: Your dad speaks Spanish?

JAYNA: Uh huh.

SHEILLA: He studied it?

JAYNA: Not really.

SHEILLA: He knows it?

JAYNA: Uh huh.

SHEILLA: How?

JAYNA: He's Mexican.

SHEILLA: *(Looking green.)* He is?

JAYNA: Born there, raised in Mexico City. He's Mexican.

SHEILLA: *(Trying to cover.)* I didn't mean . . . I mean, what I said . . . I didn't mean, um . . . Jayna I didn't . . .

JAYNA: *(Smiles, understanding the problem.)* Gotta go. See you at school. *(She takes her books and leaves.)*

(Sheilla swallows hard, sits alone, on her bed as the lights come down.)

END OF PLAY

PLAYS FOR
TWO MEN

Tennessee Ten Minute

Dan O'Brien

CHARACTERS

ART

TEN

Both could be any age, really (and any gender), though I think close to thirty-years-old would be appropriate.

SETTING

Intermediate, indeterminate; dark, dingy, two chairs and no windows.

NOTES

A slash "/" in the scripts indicates overlapping dialogue.

• • •

(An interview:)

ART: Now it says here that your name is Tennessee.

TEN: That's correct.

ART: Tennessee Williams.

TEN: That's also correct. Thank you. Yes.
    (Beat.)

ART: Now you realize, Mr. Williams, that this is a little hard to believe.

TEN: What's that.

ART: Your name.

TEN: My name is "hard to / believe — "?

ART: Yes, well, you see, there's another Tennessee Williams.
    (Beat.)

TEN: Is he a writer?

ART: He was. But he's no longer with us. He choked on a pill-bottle cap some *(Checks his wristwatch.)* twenty years ago.

TEN: I'm very sorry to hear that. . . .

ART: So you were named after him?

TEN: No, I've never met the man.

ART: All right, calm down, Mr. Williams, calm down. . . . But surely, as a playwright, as a modern American playwright, you know who Mr. Williams/ is—

TEN: I didn't name myself, you know.

ART: So you were named Tennessee at birth? — Not even Tennessee was named Tennessee at birth. Perhaps your parents—?

TEN: My parents were illiterate shepherds.

ART: Were they?

TEN: When a sheep was lost they searched for him in the high rocky places. And when they found him they carried him home triumphantly upon their backs. . . .

ART: They were patrons of the arts.

TEN: They were Americans.

(Art checks his watch.)

TEN: *(Continued.)* . . . Don't you want to hear more about my childhood?

ART: So you're saying that your parents didn't know who Tennessee Williams was?

TEN: — Absolutely not. They never left the Ozarks.

ART: But the Ozarks aren't even in Tennessee.

TEN: . . . They're not?

ART: No.

TEN: Well, my parents didn't know that.

(Beat.)

ART: I think you're having me on, Mr. Williams!

TEN: I most certainly am not!

ART: Perhaps you're the reincarnation of the late great Tennessee Williams? Have you ever thought of that?

TEN: *(Thinking of it.)* No, I can't say that I have. . . .

ART: A lot of similarities here, between you and Mr. Williams.

TEN: Like what?

ART: Well, you were born in 1973?

TEN: But that was ten years before Tennessee choked on that pill cap and died.

ART: Yes but everyone knows he was artistically dead by '61—so *(Calculating.)* yes . . . yes . . . it's *possible* . . .

TEN: I'd rather talk about myself, Mr.—

ART: Miller. Arthur Miller.

(Beat.)

ART: *(Continued.)* But you can call me Art.

Why are you looking like / that?

TEN: No reason.

ART: Is it something about my name? something in my name struck you as funny? — It's a common enough name, you know, "Miller," but so was Shakespeare and Jesus and they did all right by themselves.

TEN: Where are you from, Mr. Miller?

ART: — Oh, I see now turning the table on me are we, well: I'm from Hastings.

TEN: Hastings?

ART: -on-Hudson, yes, a wealthy suburban enclave of New York / City—

TEN: But that's not where Mr. Miller / is from—

ART: How's that?

(Beat.)

ART: *(Continued.)* Who . . . ?

(Beat.)

TEN: I've heard of Hastings-on-Hudson.

ART: You've heard of Hastings-on-Hudson but you've never heard of Tennessee—?

TEN: I dated a girl from Hastings once.

ART: Did you?

TEN: Is that so hard to believe?

ART: Frankly, Mr. Williams, it is.

TEN: She wasn't my type: stuck-up, too rich —

ART: Too Jewish . . . ?

TEN: — Don't be disgusting!

ART: You're not also an anti-Semite then, too?

TEN: "Too"? — in addition to what exactly are you / insinuating?

ART: Well I'm only inferring from your soft Southern charms —

TEN: If you're asking me if I've spent some time along the waterfront, the answer is that it was very foggy that night.

ART: Now we're getting somewhere . . .

TEN: But I always came home to my sister.

If you catch my drift.

ART: I'm afraid I don't, Mr. Williams, I'm afraid I do not. This is all getting confusing. . . .

TEN: I'll slow down.

ART: — Do you have a sister?

TEN: Why do you ask?

ART: Let me guess:

TEN: Be my guest:

ART: She's crackers.

(Ten tries to hit Art. But Art evades. A pathetic scuffle.)

ART: *(Continued.)* — Is that it, Mr. Williams? your sister is insane? and you feel a deep-bodied kinship with her and in the crucible of your writing seek to burn off the vapors of your own encroaching insanity?

TEN: *(Sitting, exhausted.)* . . . I'm not sure I feel I know you well enough . . .

ART: . . . I am a writer, Mr. Williams. — I, Arthur Miller, am also a writer. And I know what grist we writers must needs make of our own personal trauma.

TEN: — What do you have to complain about?

ART: I don't think this is supposed to be about me.

TEN: Isn't it . . . ?

ART: I don't think it is . . . is it?

TEN: You're right. It's about me, it's always about me and I'd like to say that—

ART: But now that you bring it up I think you ought to know my fairly held conviction that we all like to think we're someone special but as the hydra-headed advances of the past thousand years have proved when we dig deep enough into the soft soil of the soul the psyche the self or what have you there's nothing there at all and it horrifies. Repulses. — But why be afraid? Why turn in horror from the truth? Why not embrace that and say yes that anything I know is known by everyone and everything I have ever lived through has been lived by someone first and yes much more than that I will never know? Why not surrender all pretense to the contrary and say that I am no one special?

(*Beat.*)

When I imagine my self-portrait, I picture the ocean.

(*Beat.*)

It terrifies me.

TEN: I'm a soft-spoken man.

ART: As am I, by nature. . . .

TEN: I prefer long walks in the woods, women with wide hips — *I'm a poet!* — and a religious man: cardinals in the brush, the bird not always singing but thrashing in the brush . . .

ART: I'm not sure I know what you're getting at, Mr. / Williams.

TEN: When I was a child I was a person.

When I was a child I was the only person.

One in a full but small kingdom of people.

And my mother would sing my sister to sleep.

In the dark room, my sister in her arms, starlight and moonlight and the electric orange street lamp soft upon her shoulders, and her face, singing my sister to sleep. . . .

I would wait and listen in the well-lit hallway.

Listening to that song.

And when she had finished, and lay my sister down to sleep, I would run away, so as not to be discovered.

(*Beat.*)

ART: You'll excuse me for saying this, Mr. Miller, but you seem to have come somewhat unhinged.

TEN: I'm aware of that. I'm afraid of that. I've never been very proud of that.

ART: — No, it makes me like you that much more.

TEN: Does it?

ART: It makes me feel I know you better now.

TEN: Does it do that for you? — Well!

ART: Would you like to get a drink after we're done here? We could talk about you some more.

TEN: Yes, I would like that very much. . . .

(He smiles broadly. Blackout.)

END OF PLAY

Aurolac Blues © 2006 by Saviana Stanescu. Used by permission of the author. For performance rights, contact the author at savianas@yahoo.com

Bedtime Stories © 2007 by Brian Mori. Used by permission of the author. For performance rights, contact Marta Praeger, Robert A. Freedman Dramatic Agency, 1501 Broadway #2310, New York, NY 10036. Contact the author at brmori@aol.com

Bethlehem, PA © 2004 by Suzanne Bradbeer. Used by permission of the author. For performance rights, contact the author at suzab12@aol.com

Boxes © 2007 by Wendy MacLeod. Used by permission of Beth Blickers, Abrams Artists Agency, 275 7th Ave., New York, NY 10001. For performance rights, contact Beth Blickers. beth.blickers@abramsart.com

Brother/Bar © 2005 by Jeff Tabnick. Used by permission of the author. For performance rights, contact the author at jefftabnick@yahoo.com

Cloudy © 2007 by Michael Griffo. Used by permission of Buddy Thomas, International Creative Management, 40 W. 57th St., New York, NY 10019. Contact Buddy Thomas for performance rights. bthomas@icmtalent.com

Creatrix © 2006 by Don Nigro. Used by permission of the author. For performance rights, contact the author at jnigro@neo.rr.com

Dance © 2007 by Greg Zittel. Used by permission of the author. For performance rights, contact the author at greg49@aol.com

Decoding Fruit © 2007 by Molly Smith Metzler. Used by permission of the author. For performance rights, contact Maura Teitelbaum at Abrams Artists, 275 7th Ave., New York, NY 1000. maura.teitelbaum@abramsart.com

Different © 2004 by Lisa Soland. Used by permission of the author. For performance rights, contact the author at lisasoland@aol.com

The First Time Out of Bounds © 2006 by P. Seth Bauer. Used by permission of the author. For performance rights, contact Marta Praeger, Robert A. Freedman Dramatic Agency, 1501 Broadway #2310, New York, NY 10036.

5G/10B © 2007 by Michael Griffo. Used by permission of the author. For performance rights, contact the author at michaelgriffo@hotmail.com

Foul Territory © 2003 by Craig Wright. Used by permission of Beth Blickers, Abrams Artists Agency, 275 7th Ave., New York, NY 10001. For performance rights, contact Beth Blickers. beth.blickers@abramsart.com

The Ghost of Red Roses © 2007 by David Cirone. Used by permission of Buddy Thomas, International Creative Management, Inc., 40 W. 57th Street, New York, NY 10019. For performance rights, contact Buddy Thomas. bthomas@icmtalent.com

Halasana © 2007 by Kayla Cagan. Used by permission of the author. For performance rights, contact the author at kayla.cagan@gmail.com